Copyright © 2017 by Tyeesha Bradley
All rights reserved. No part of this publication may be reproduced, distributed or transmitted in any form or by any means, including photocopying, recording, or other electronic or mechanical methods, without the prior written permission of the publisher, except in the case of brief quotations embodied in critical reviews and certian other noncommercial uses permitted by copyright law.

Ordering Information
This coloring book is available for purchase on Amazon.com and Etsy.com

Au Naturale: An Adult Coloring Book/ Tyeesha Bradley. - 1st ed.

To my husband Phil. For being my motivator, coach, and my accountabila-buddy. thank you so much, I love you babe

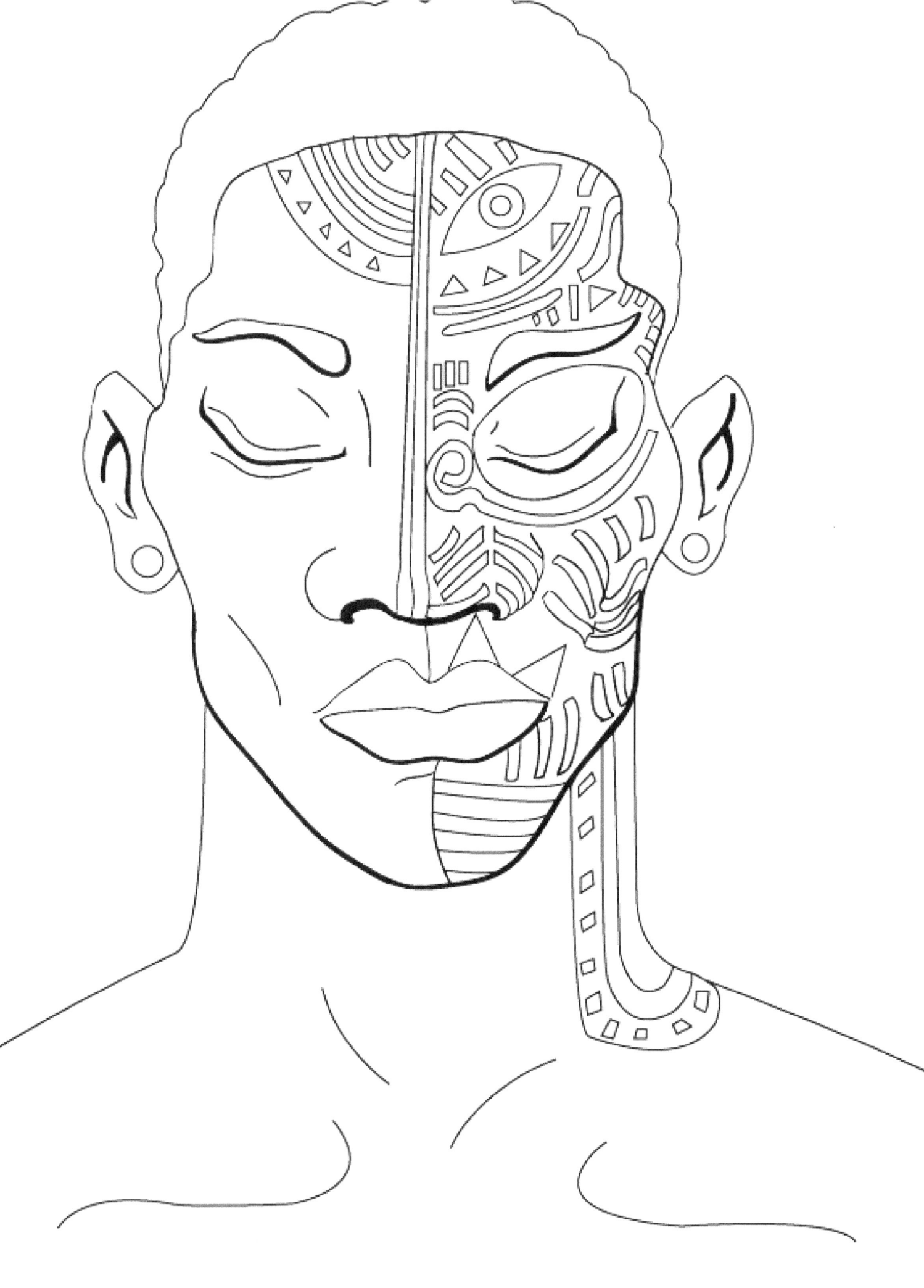

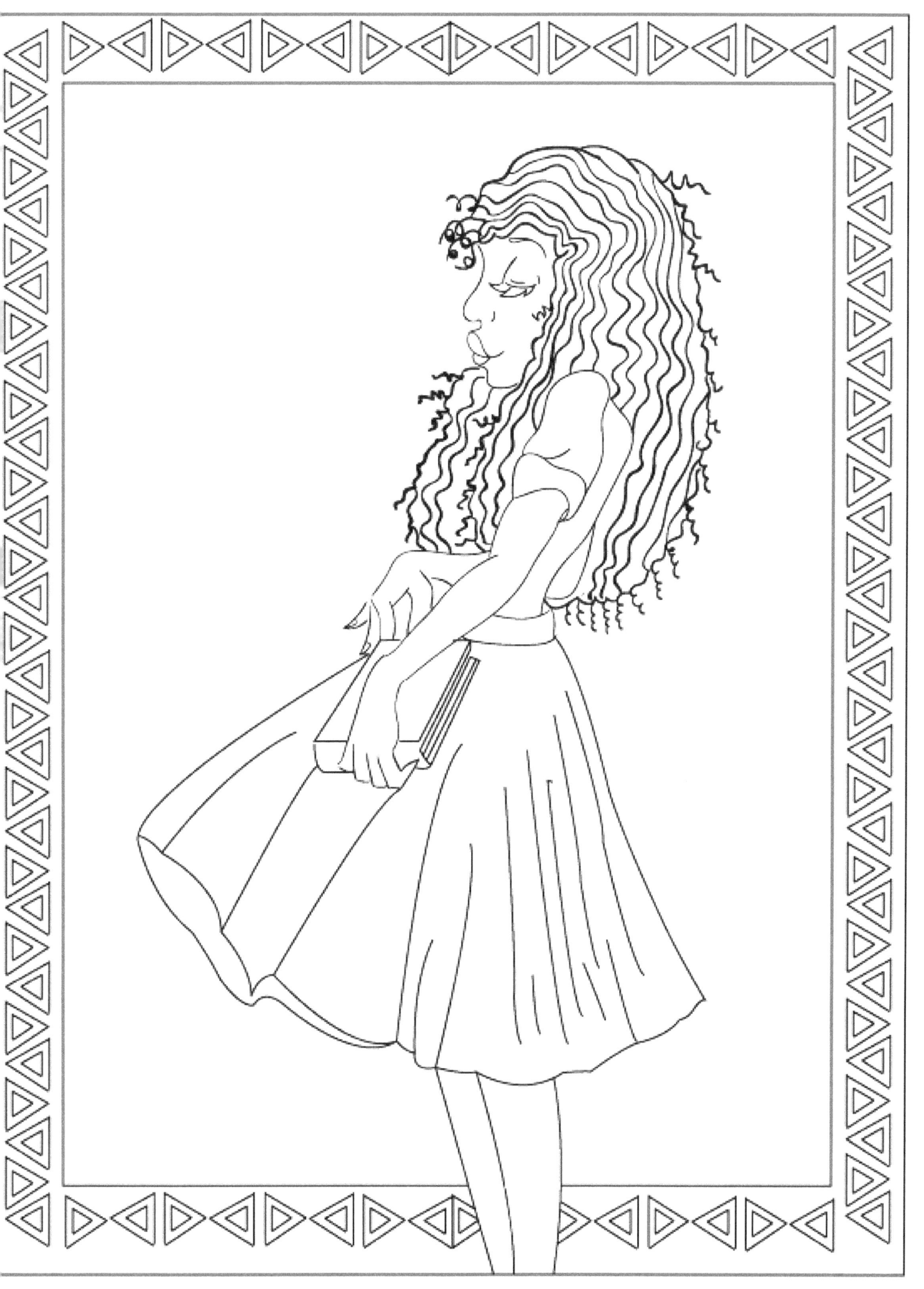

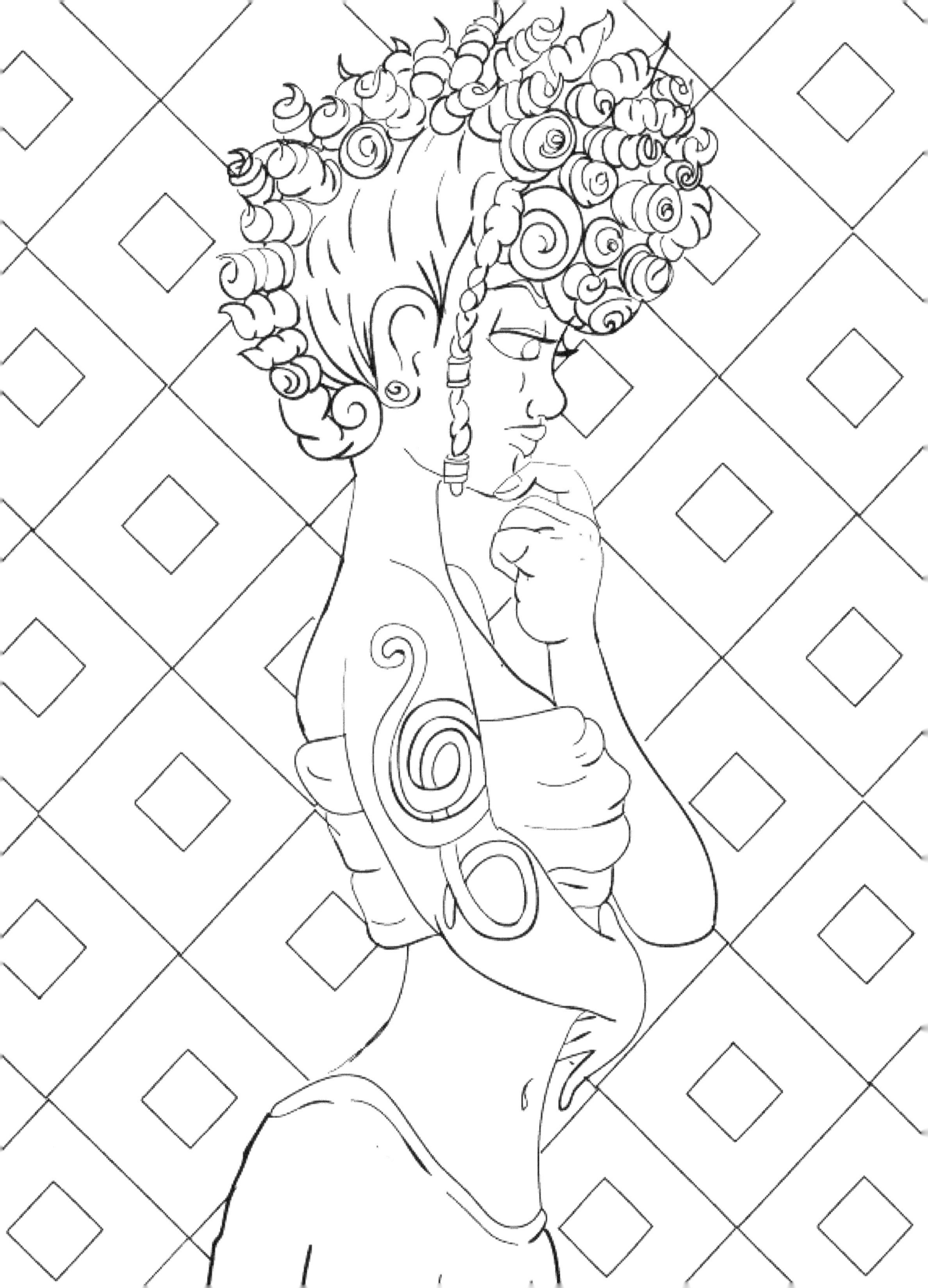

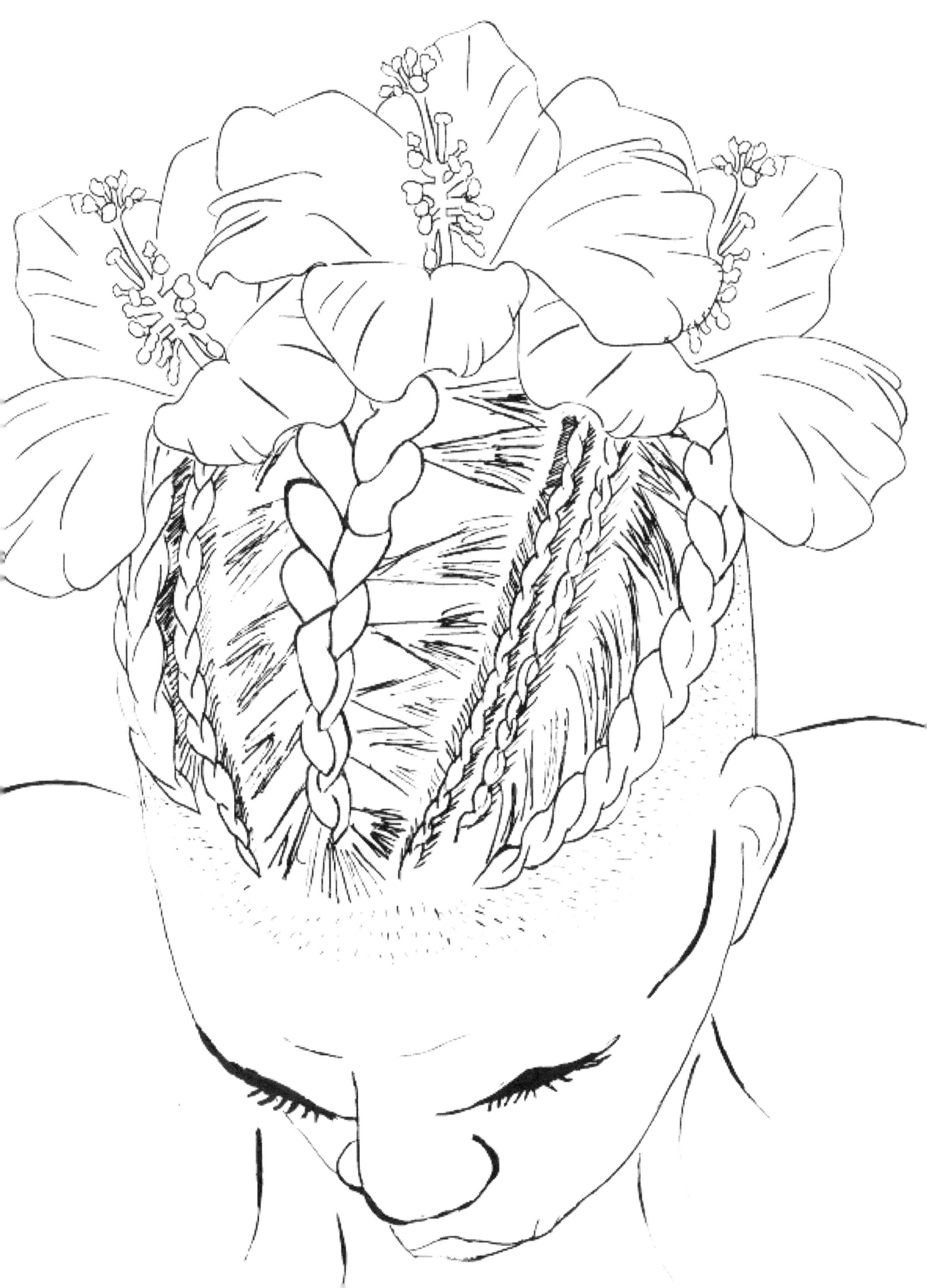

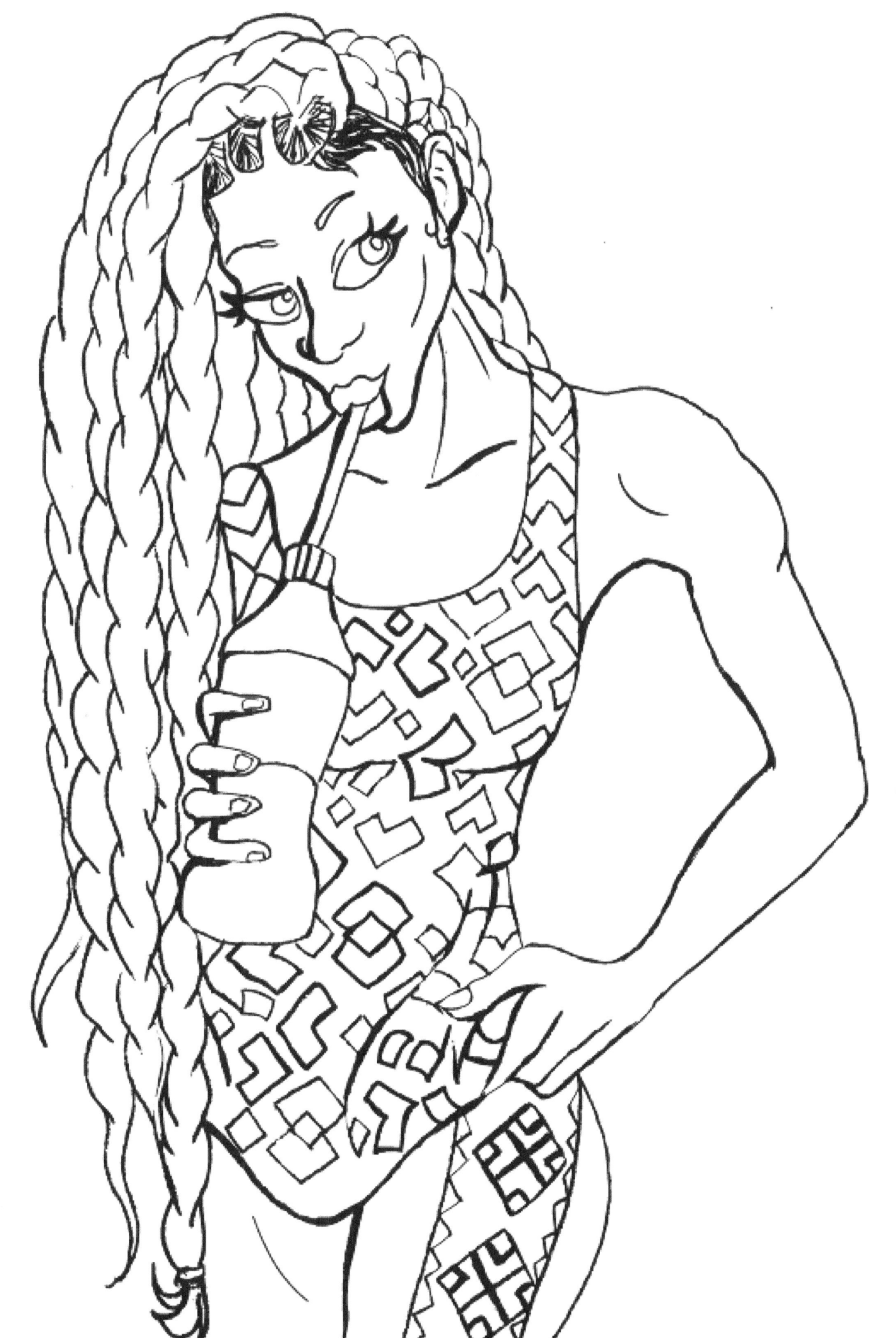

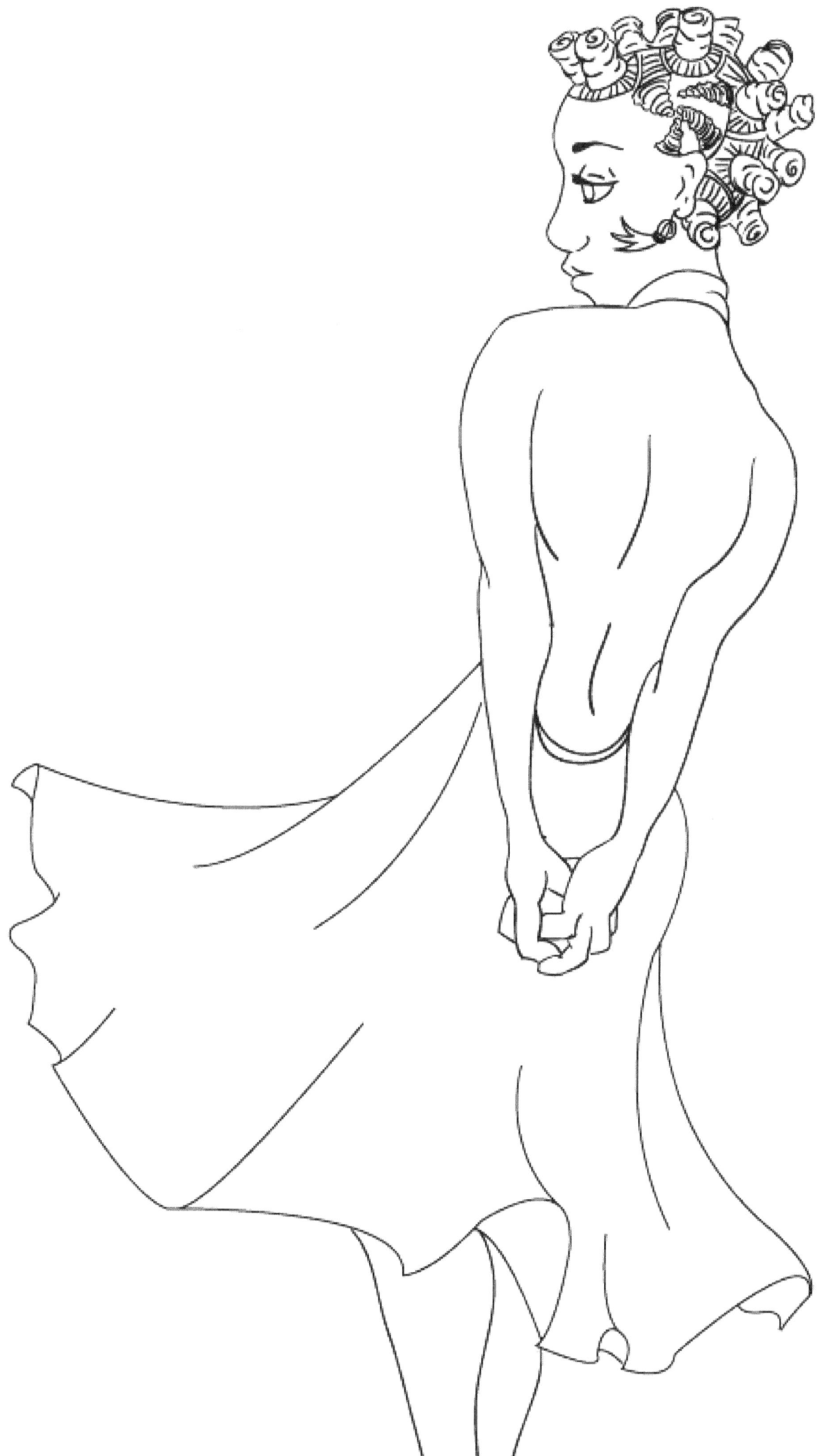

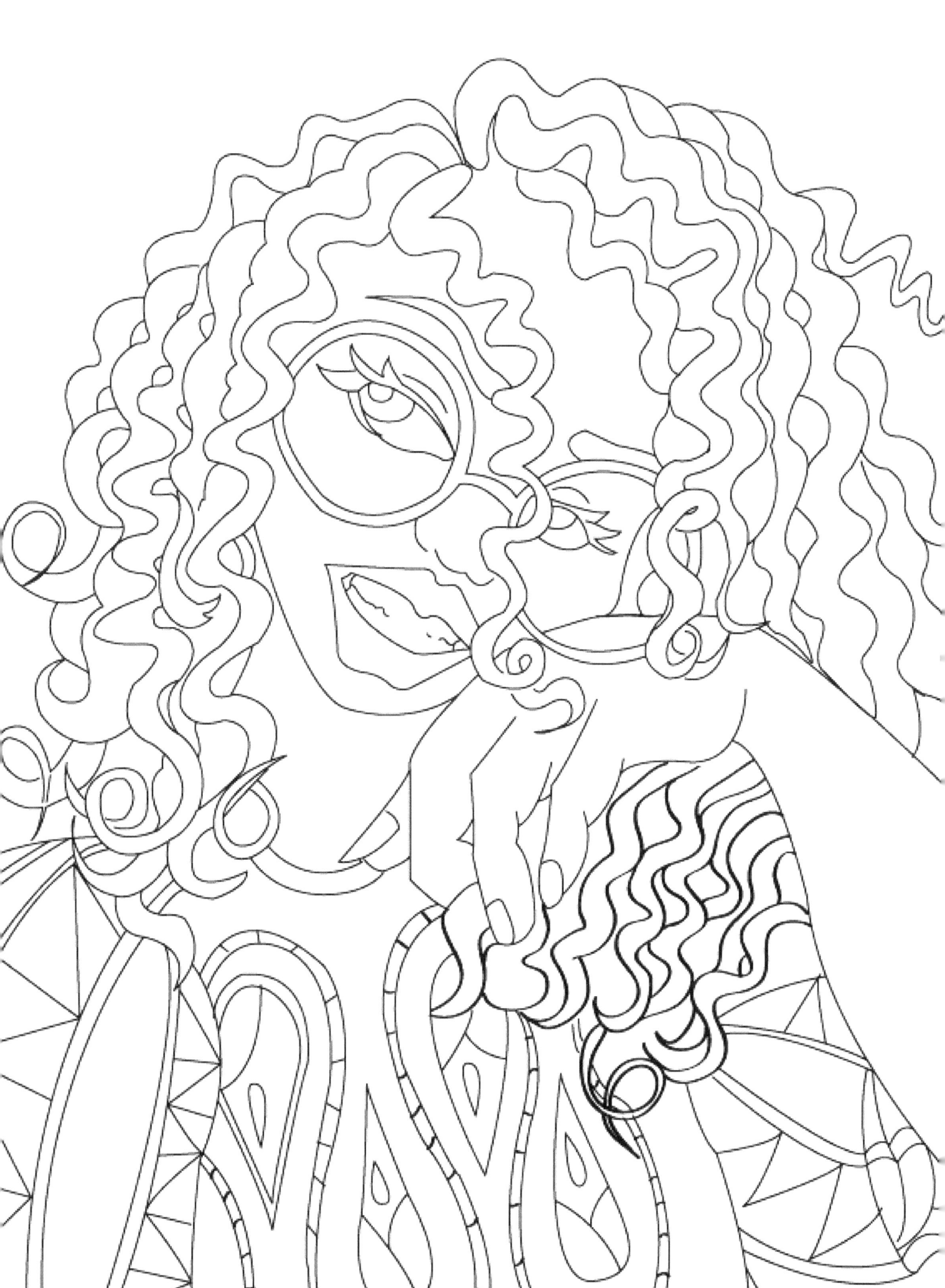

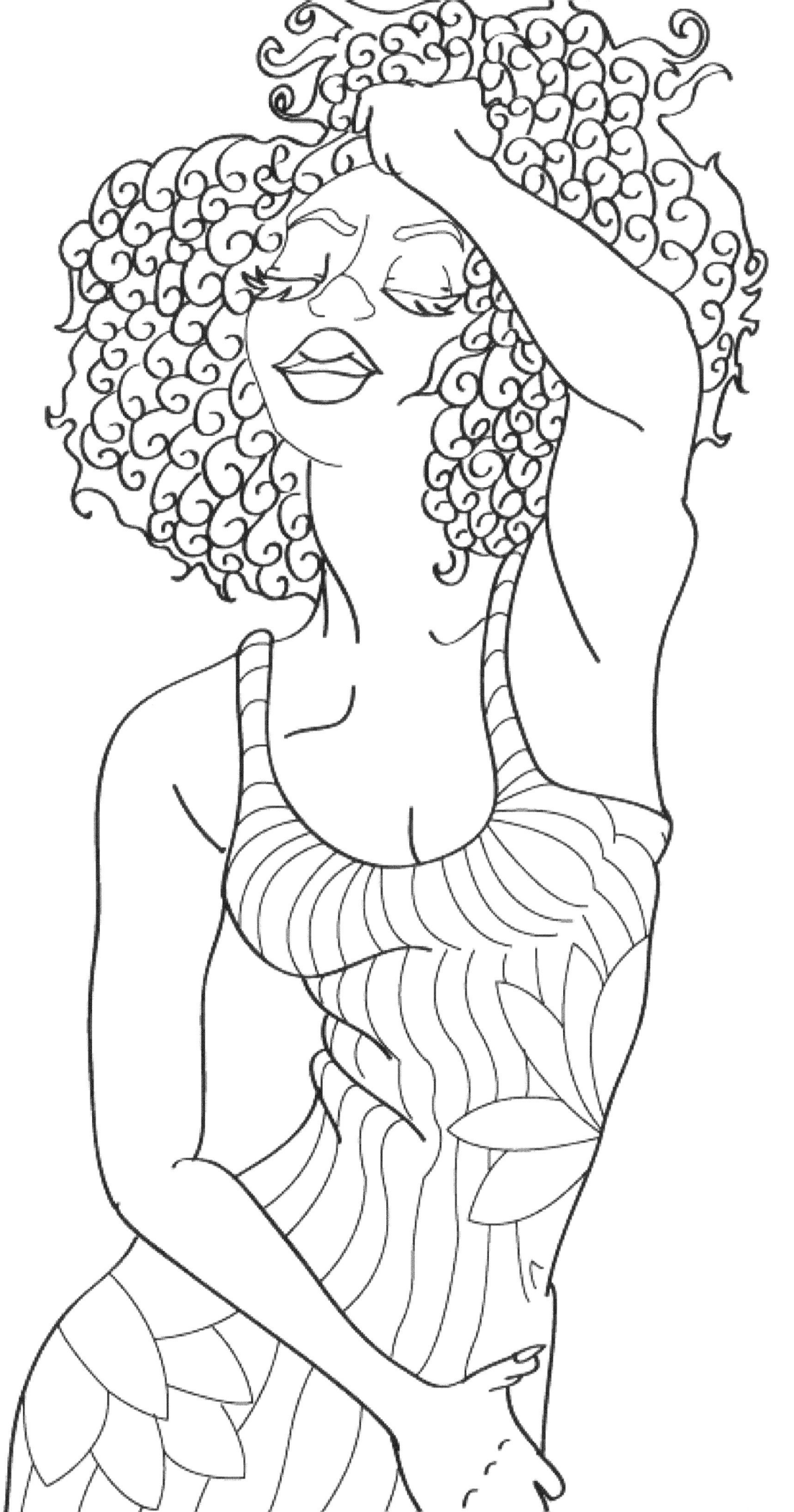

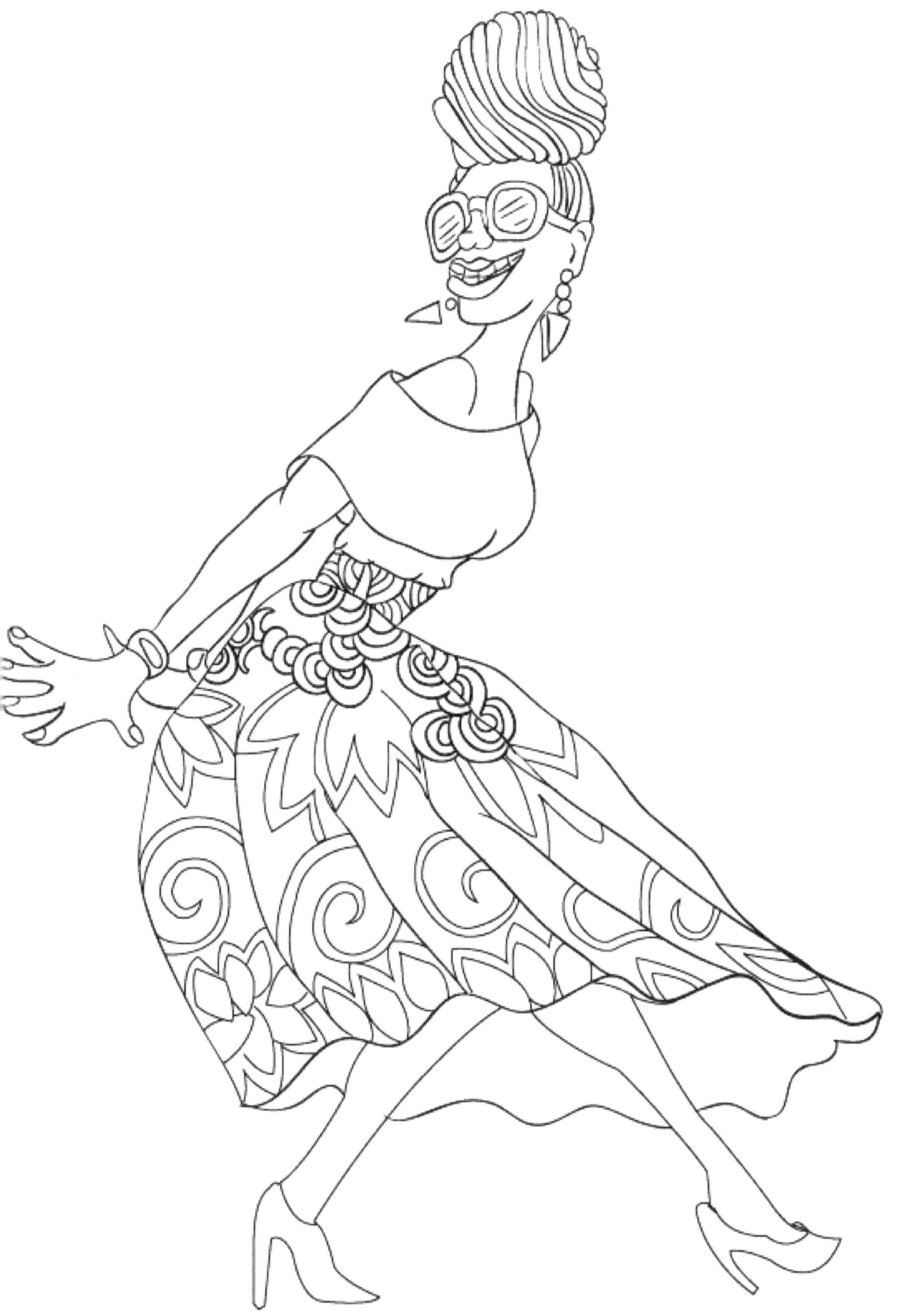

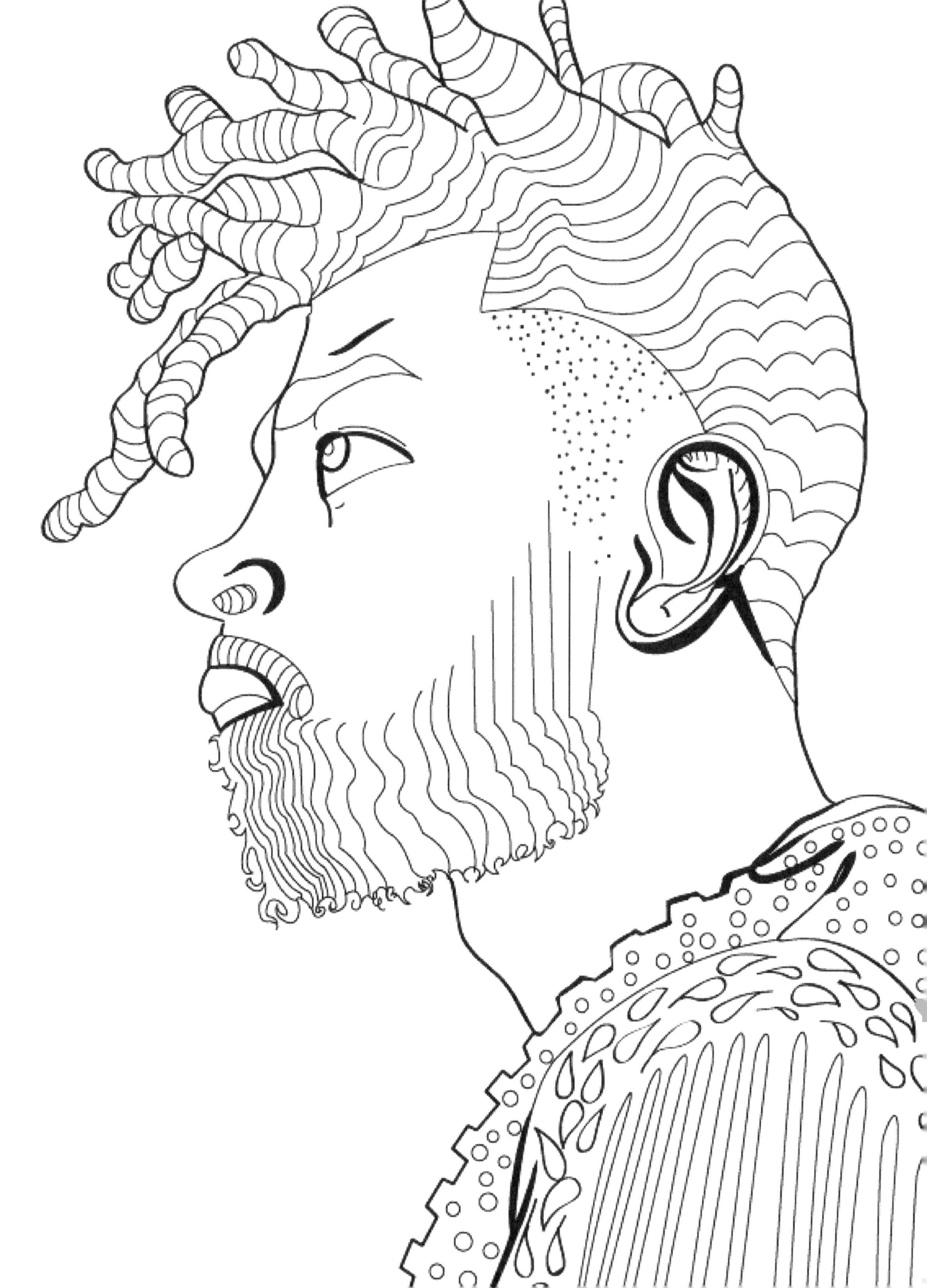

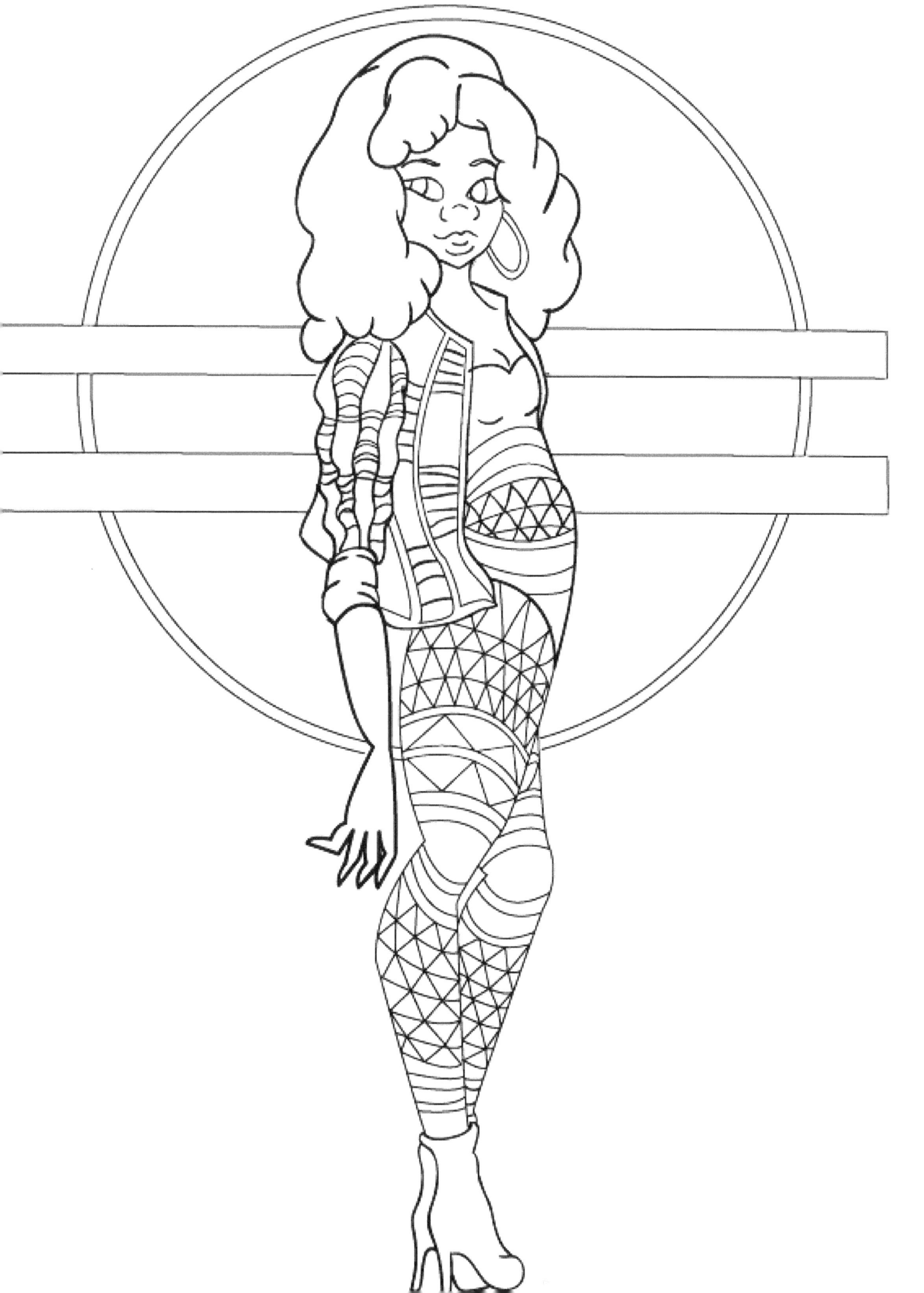

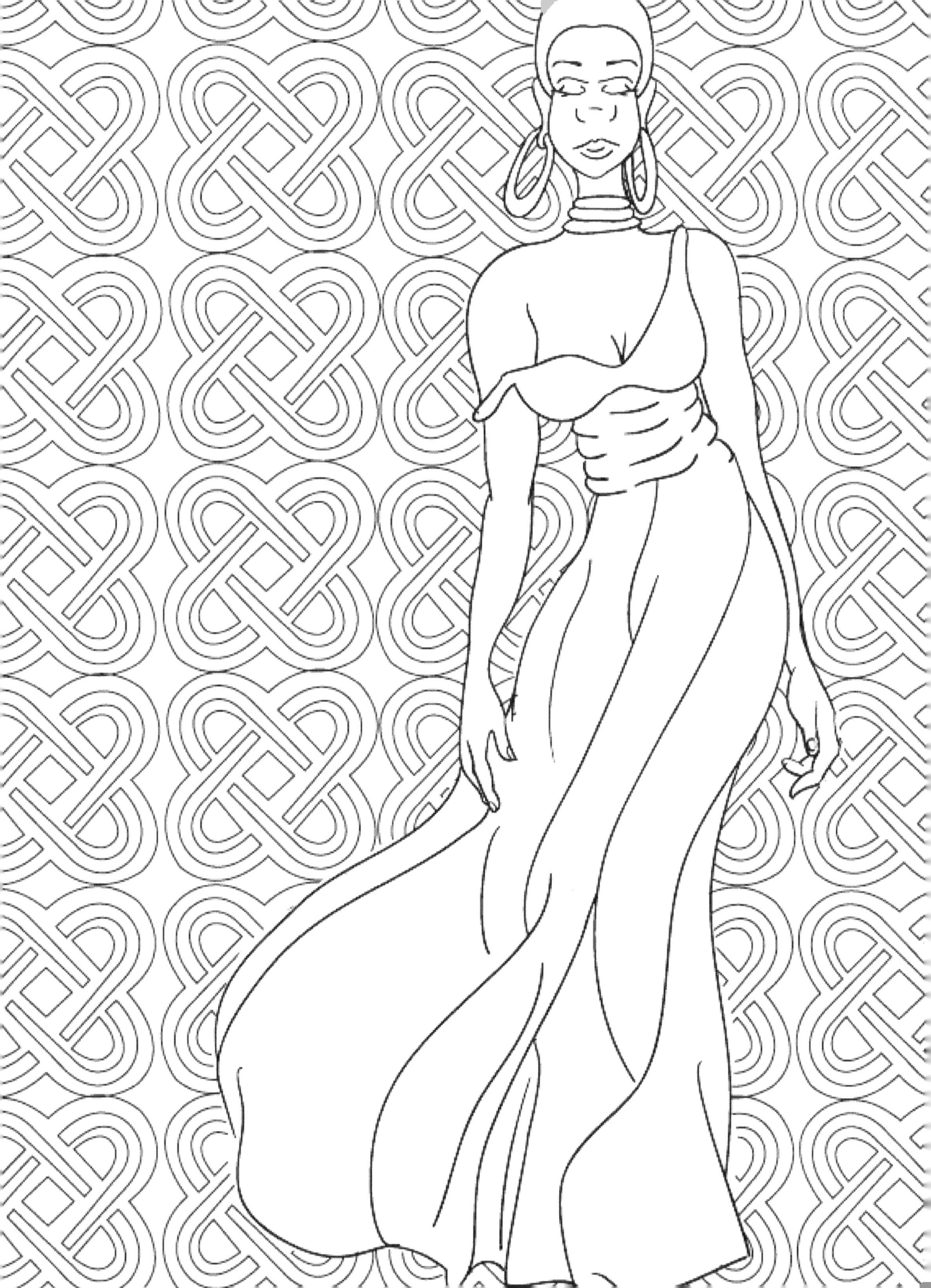

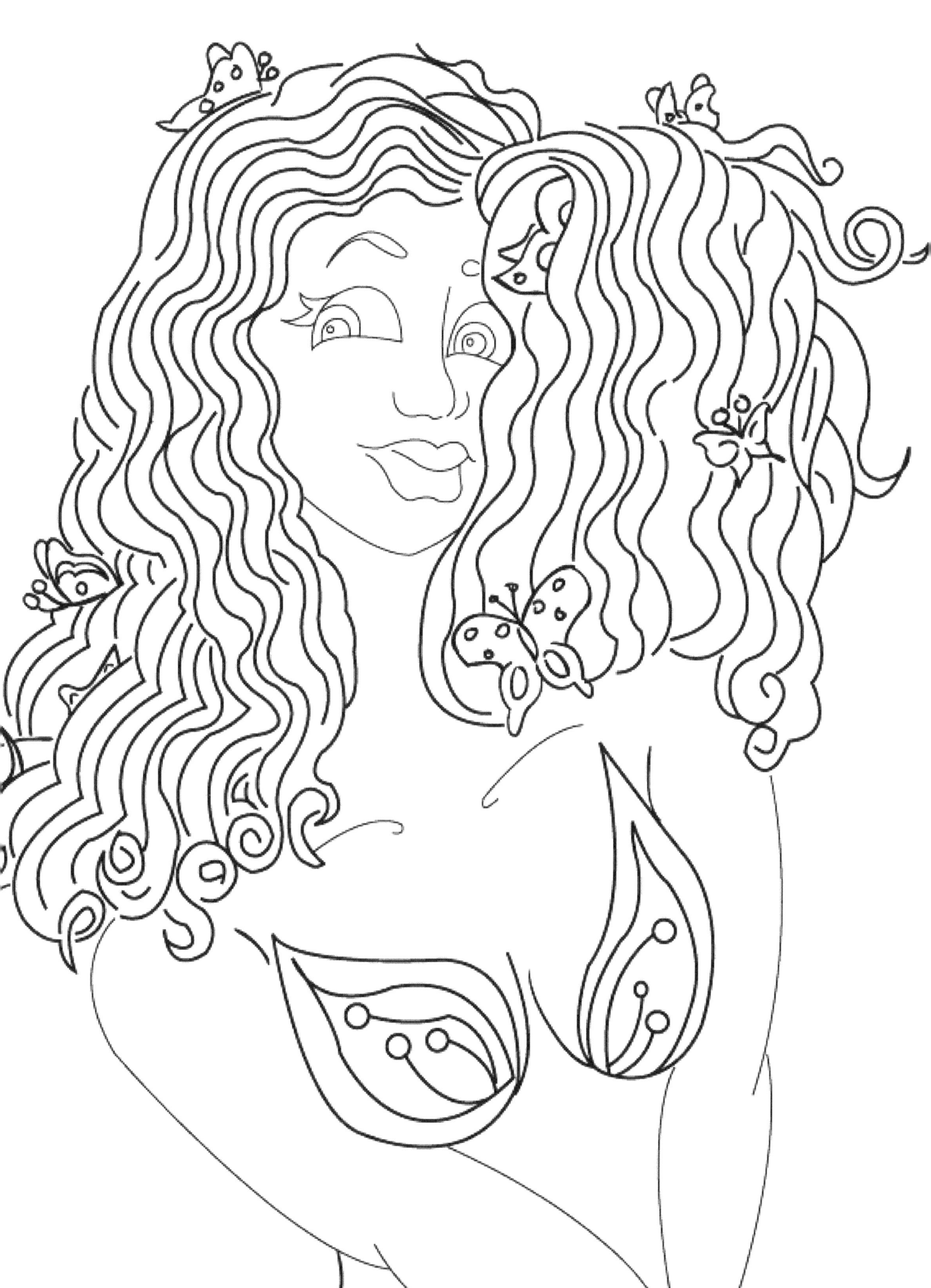

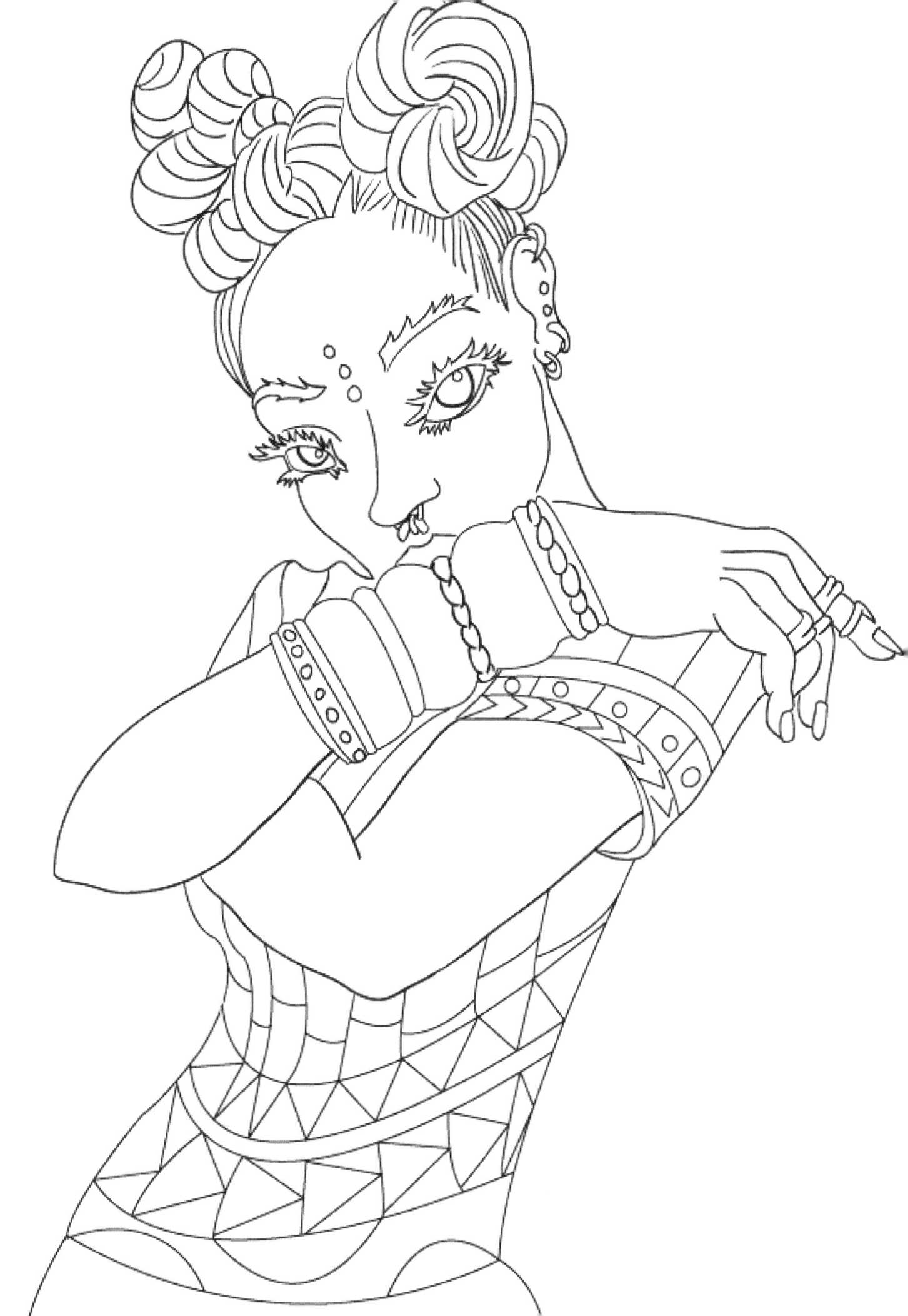

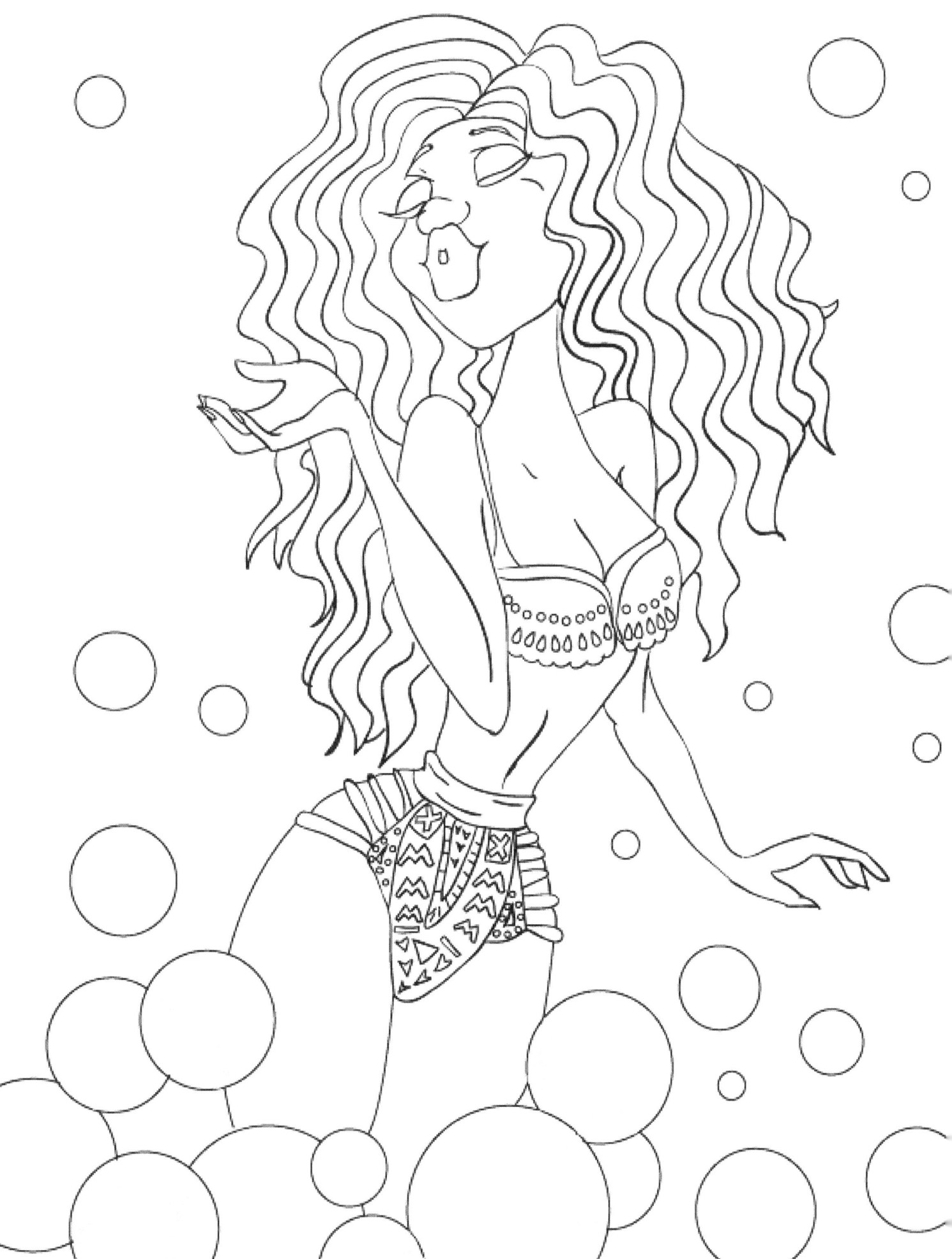

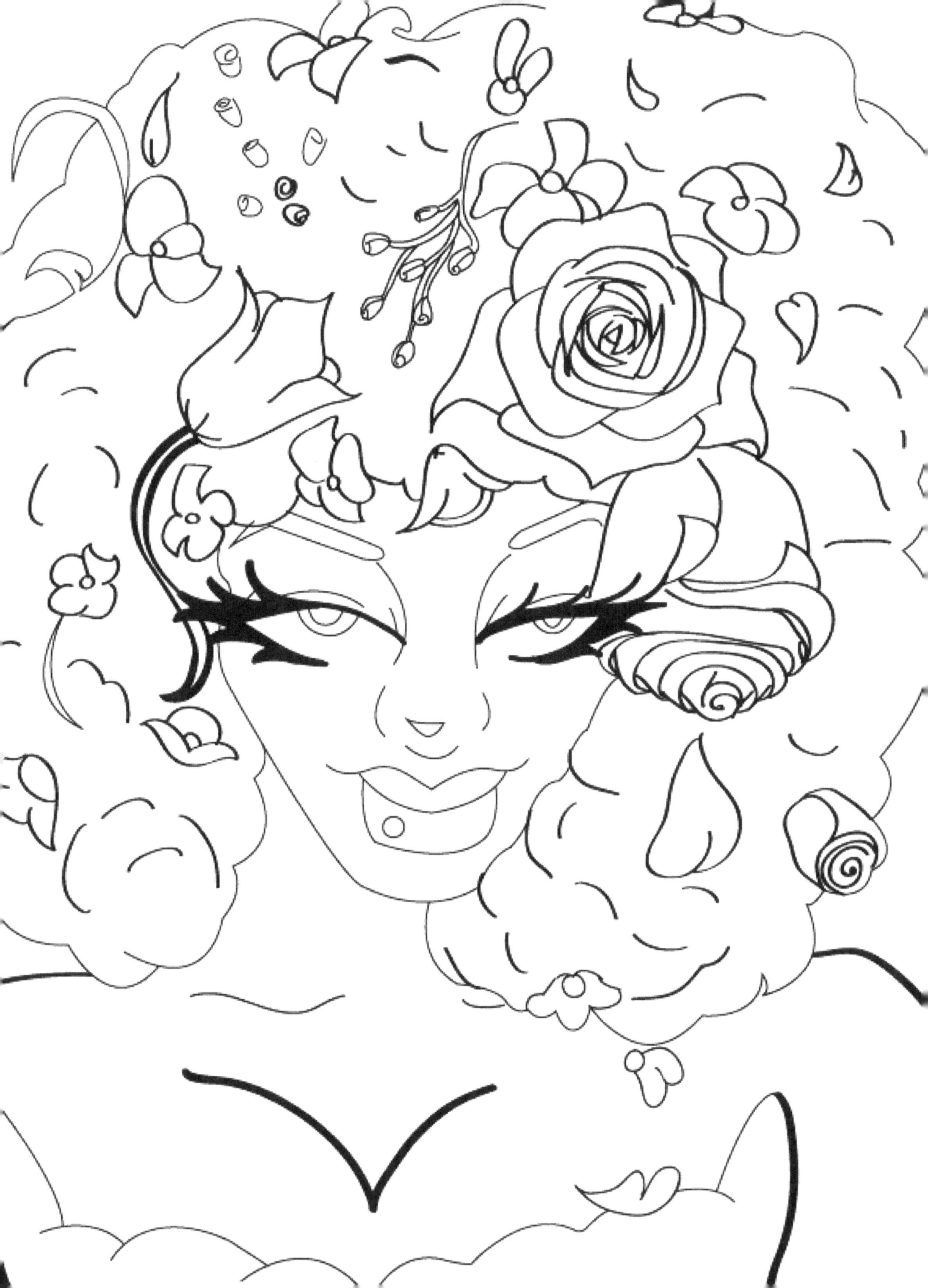

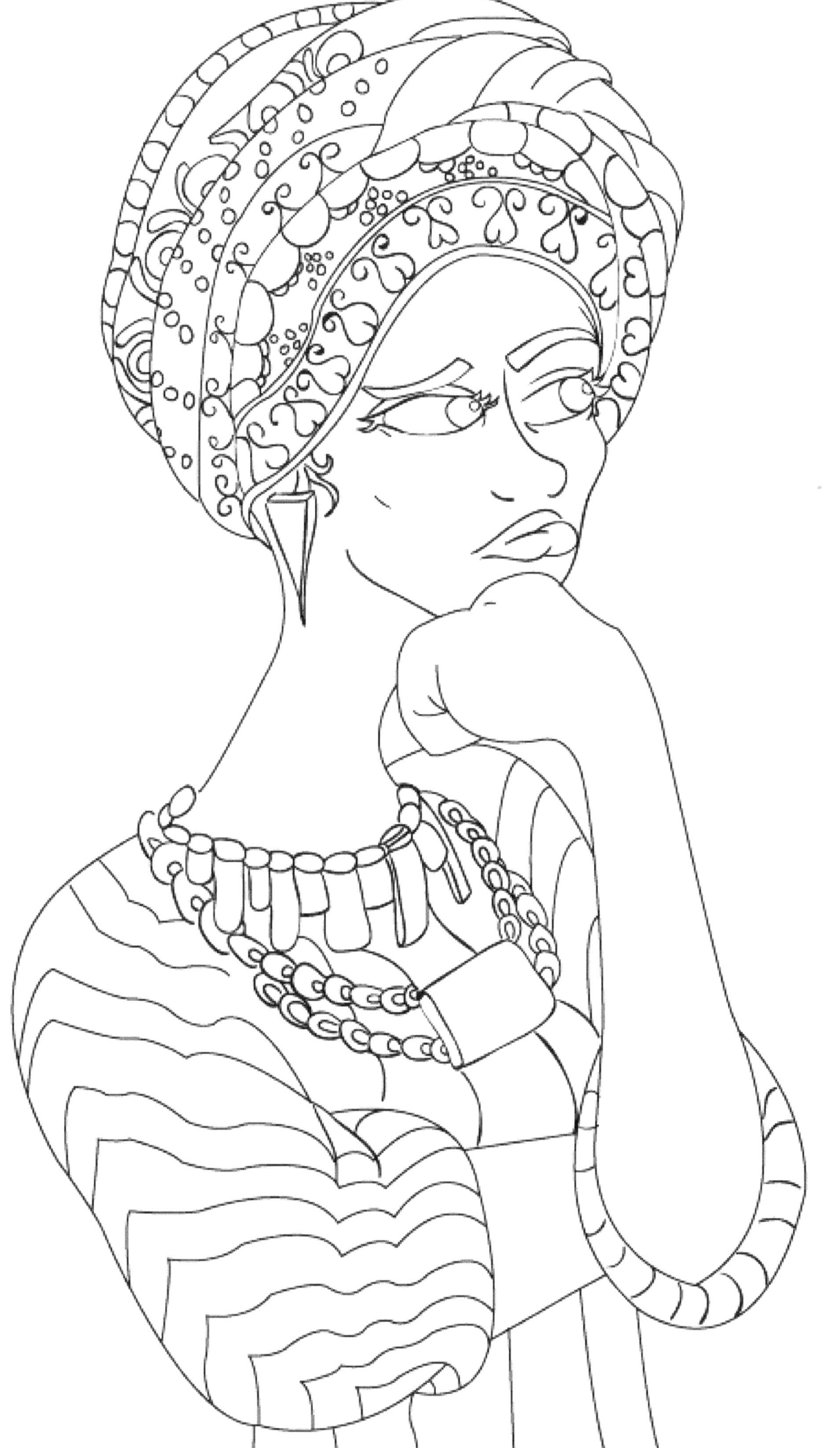

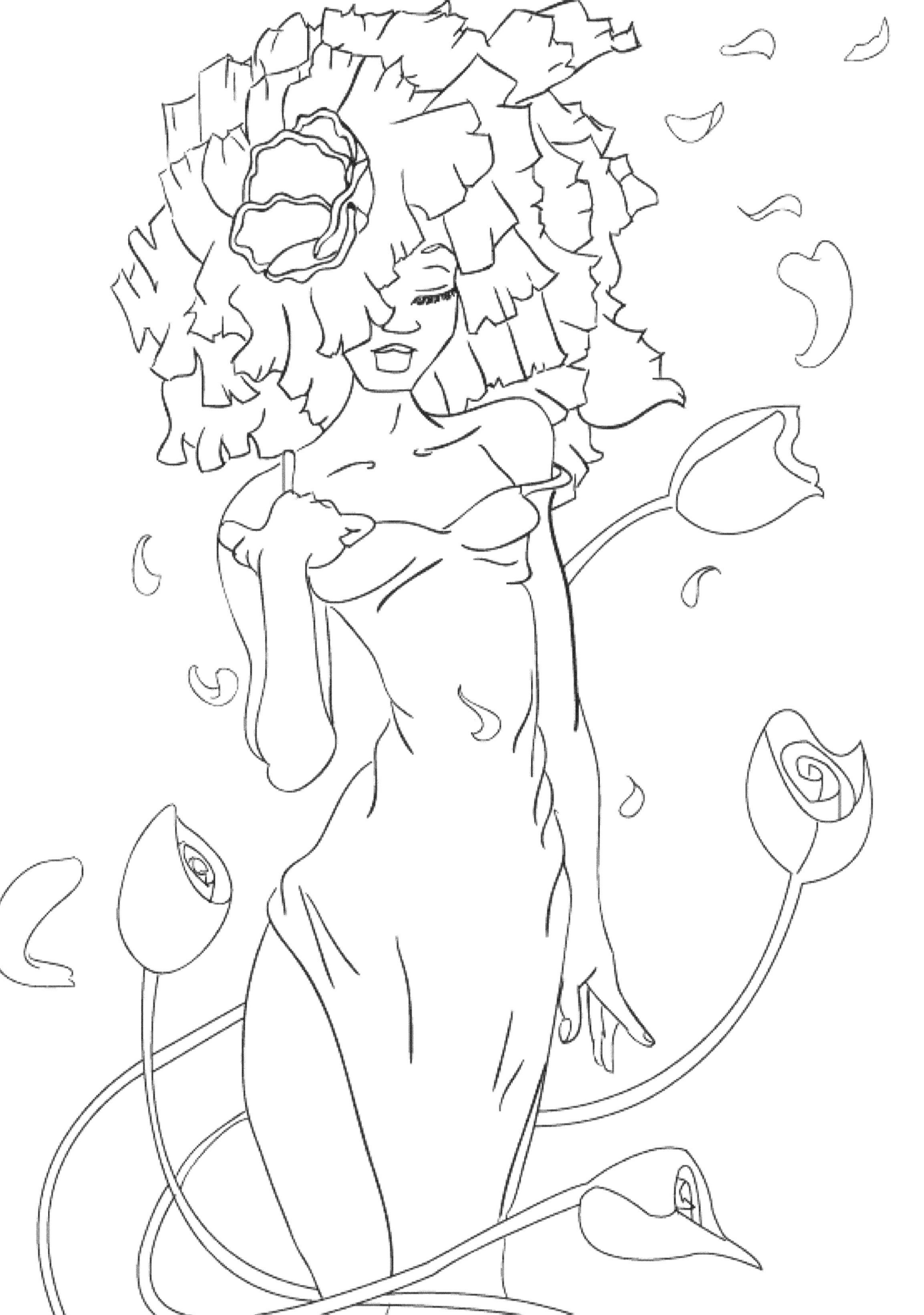

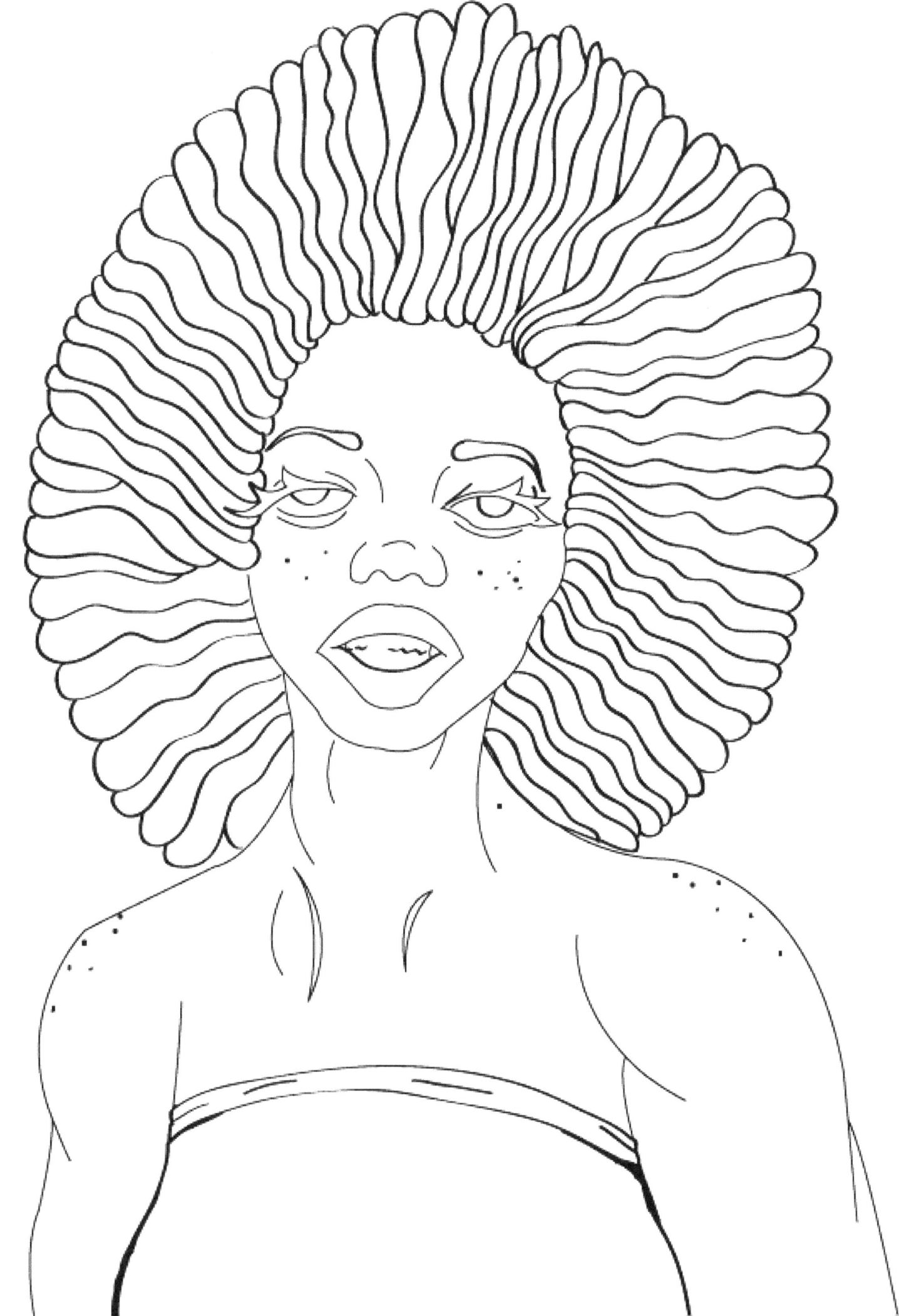

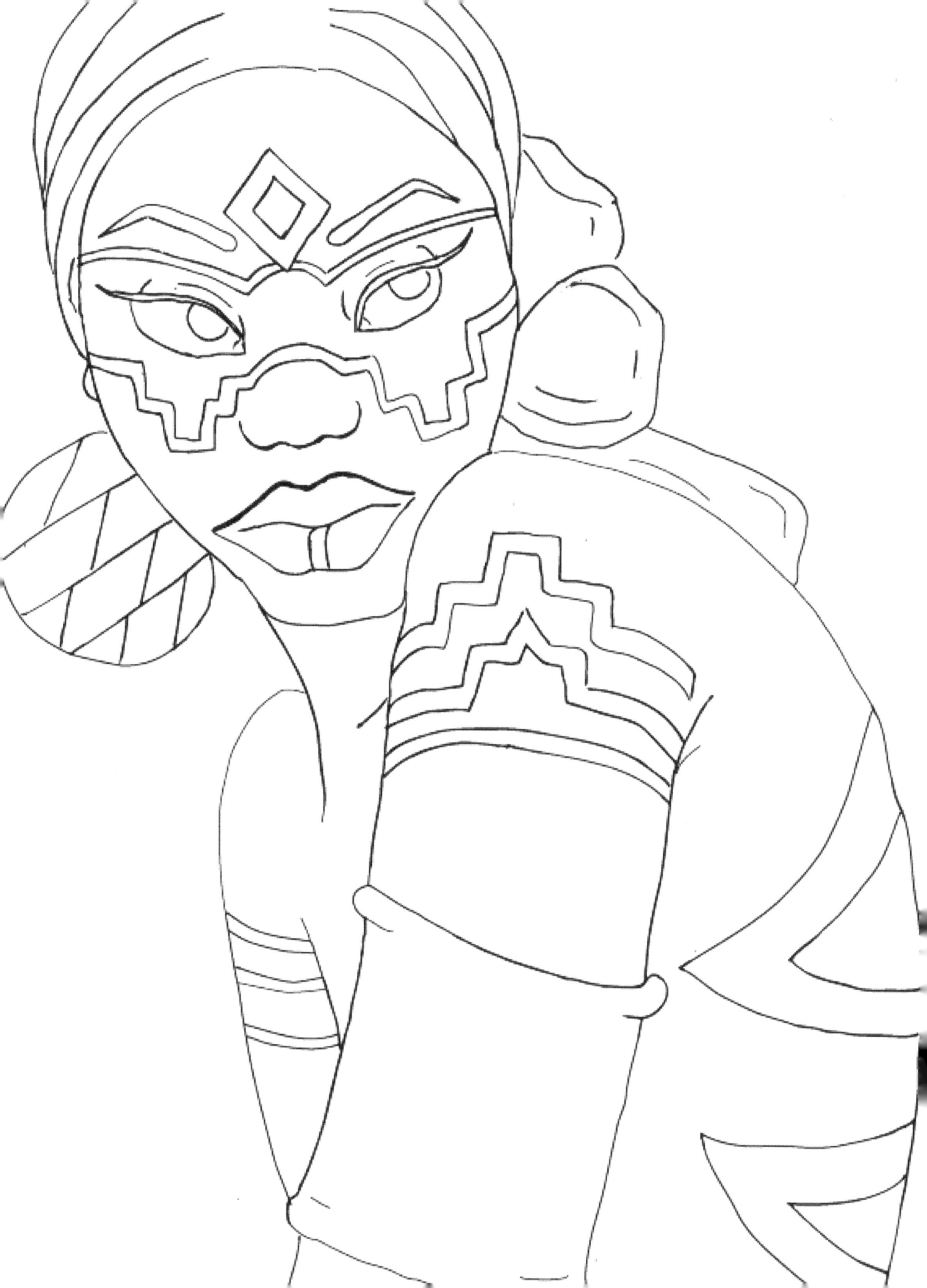

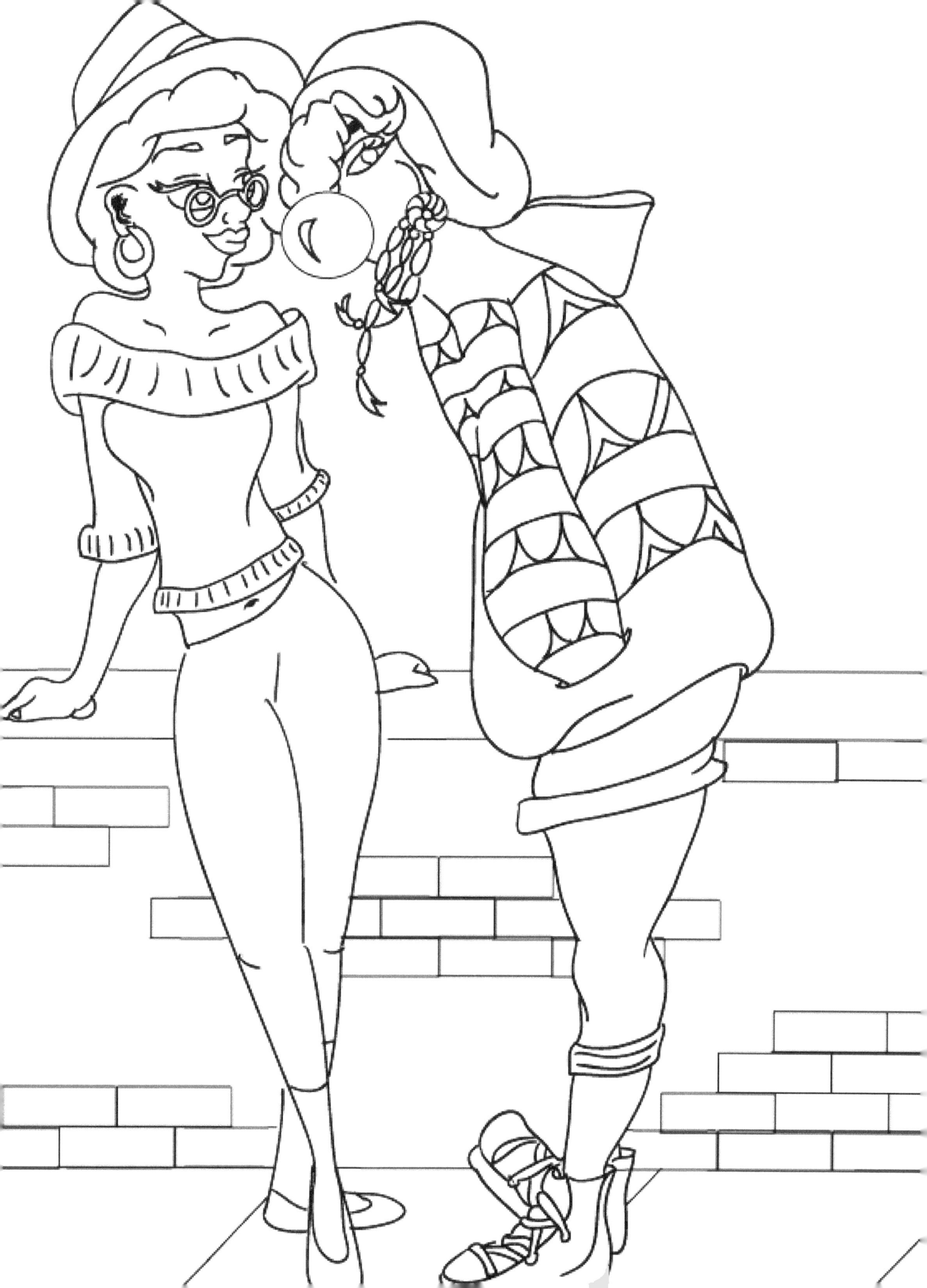

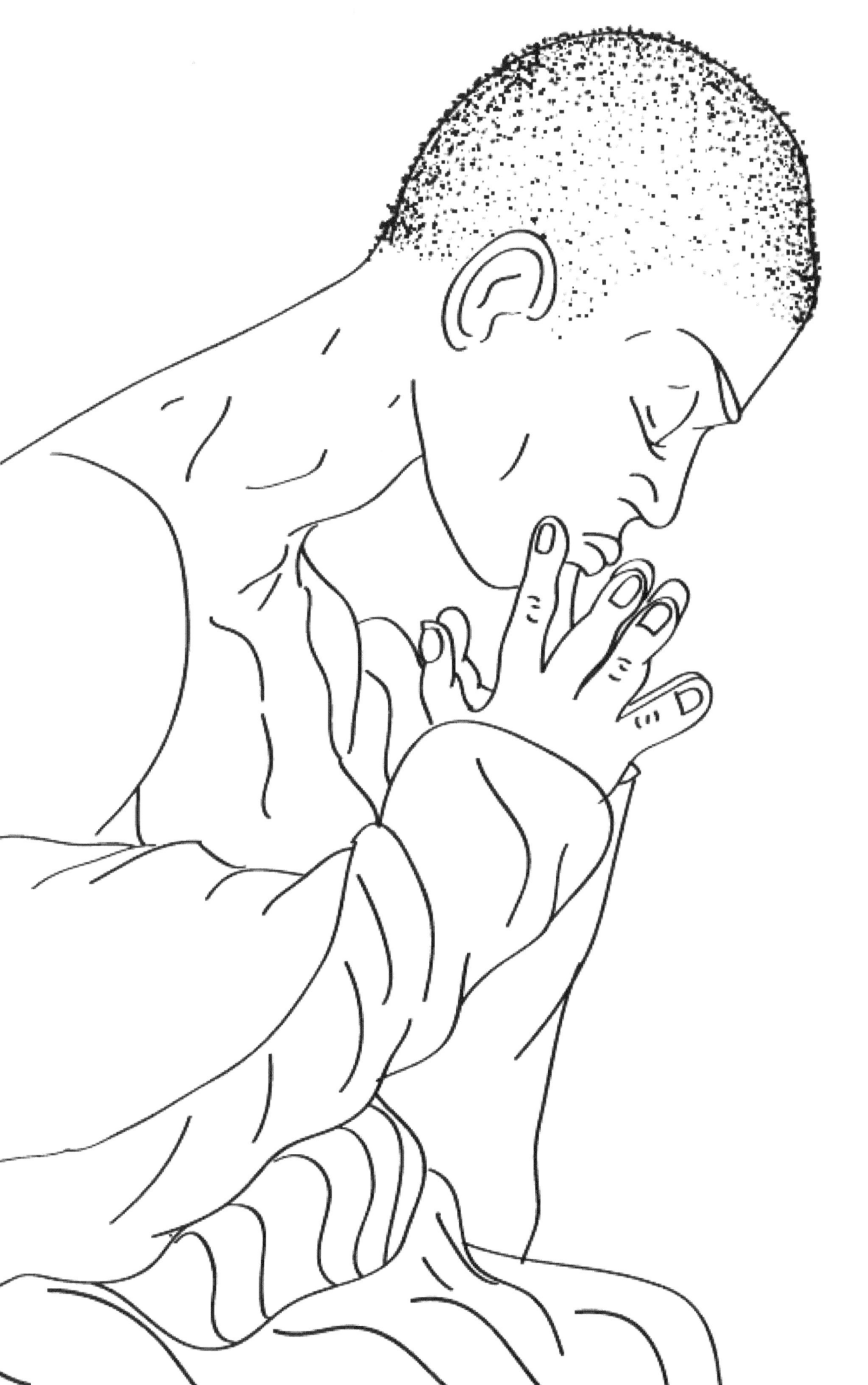

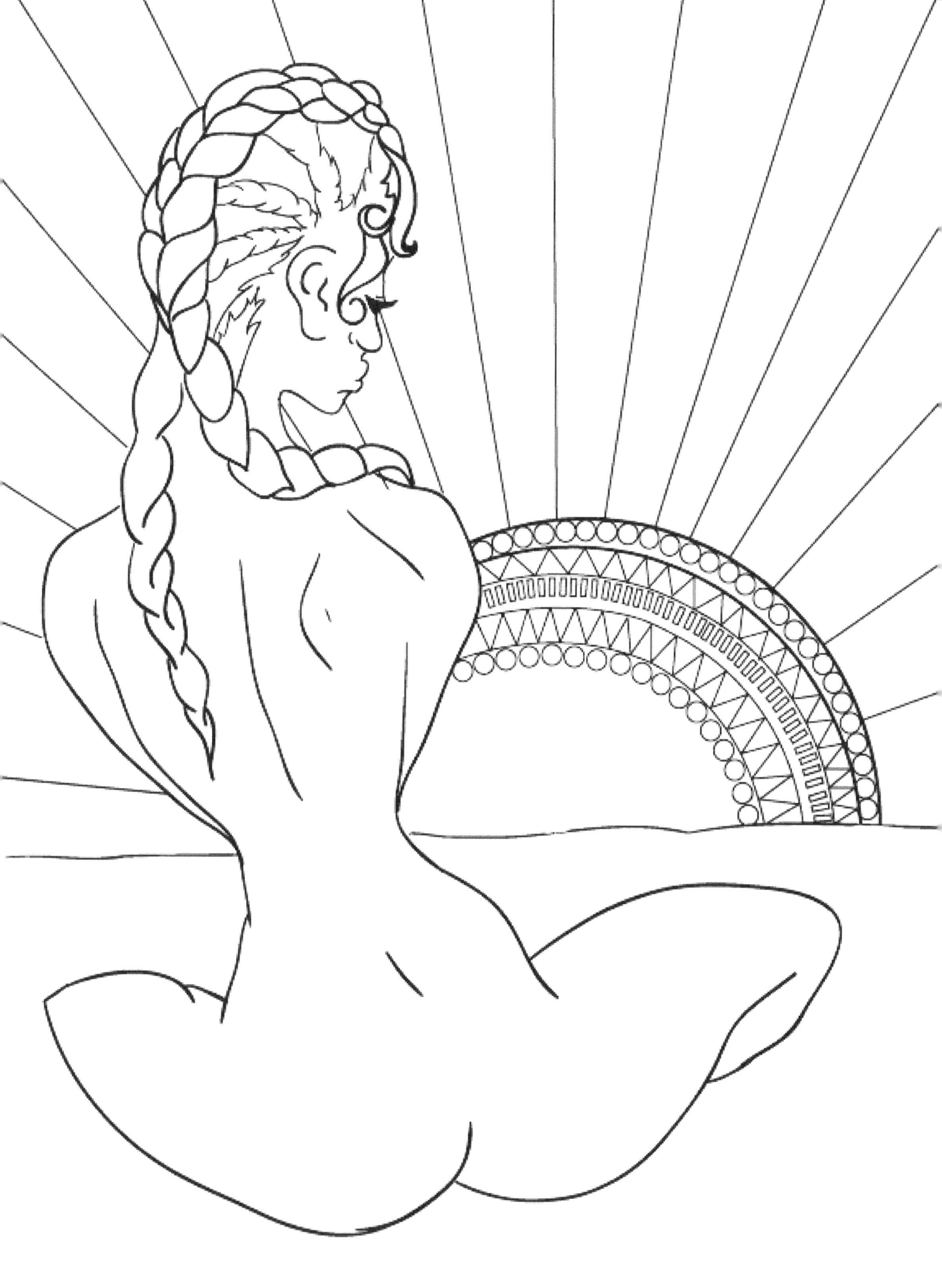

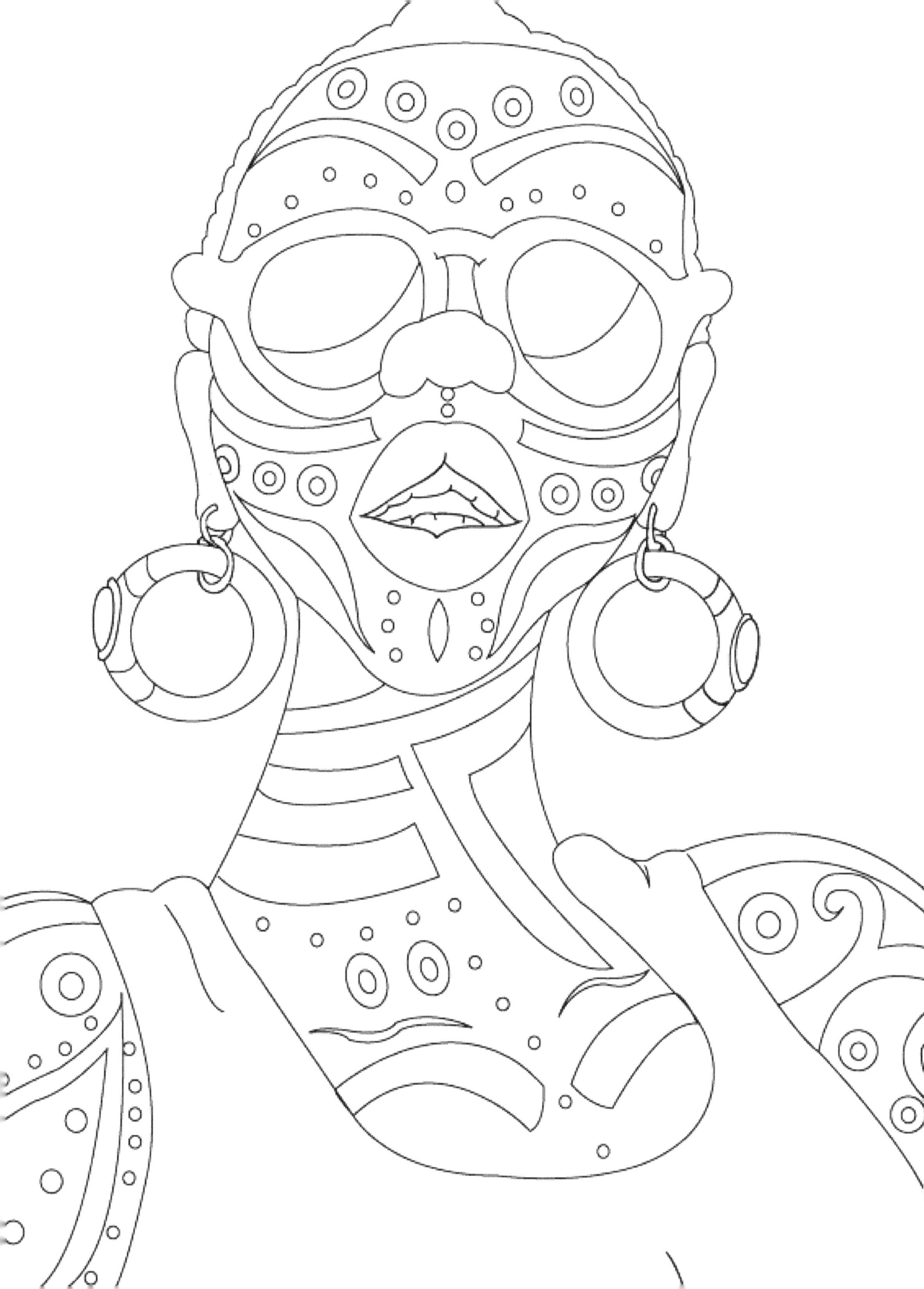

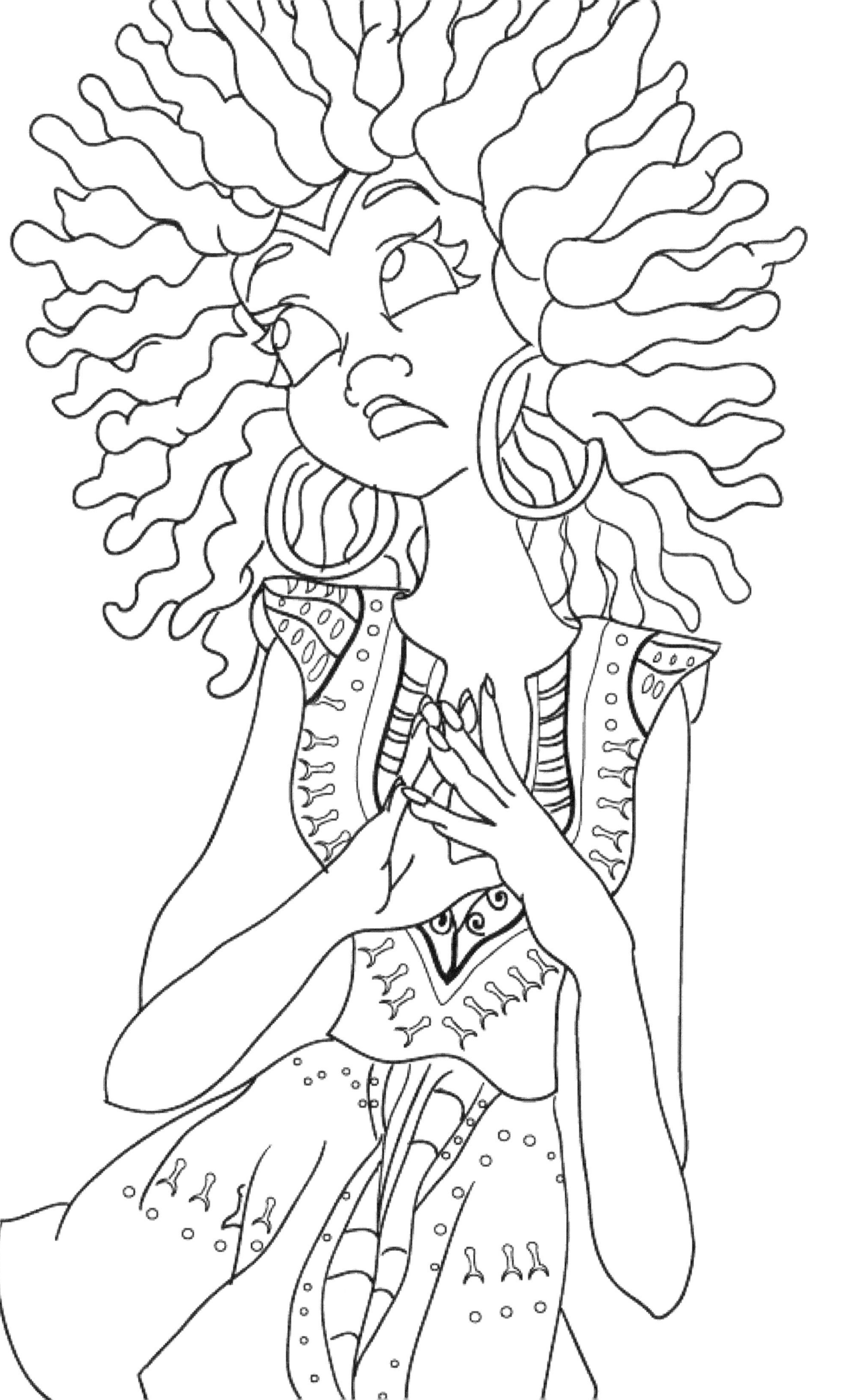

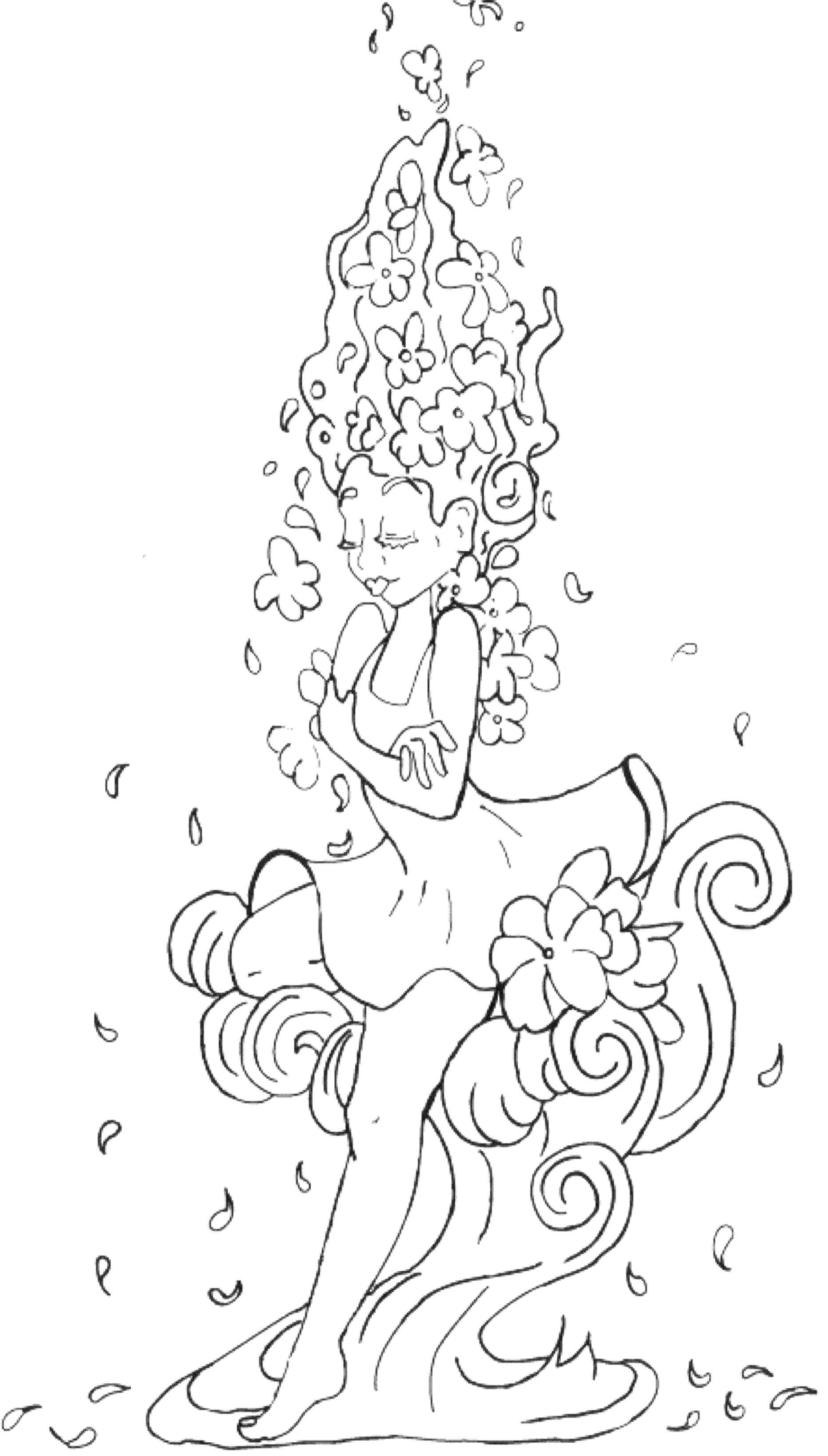

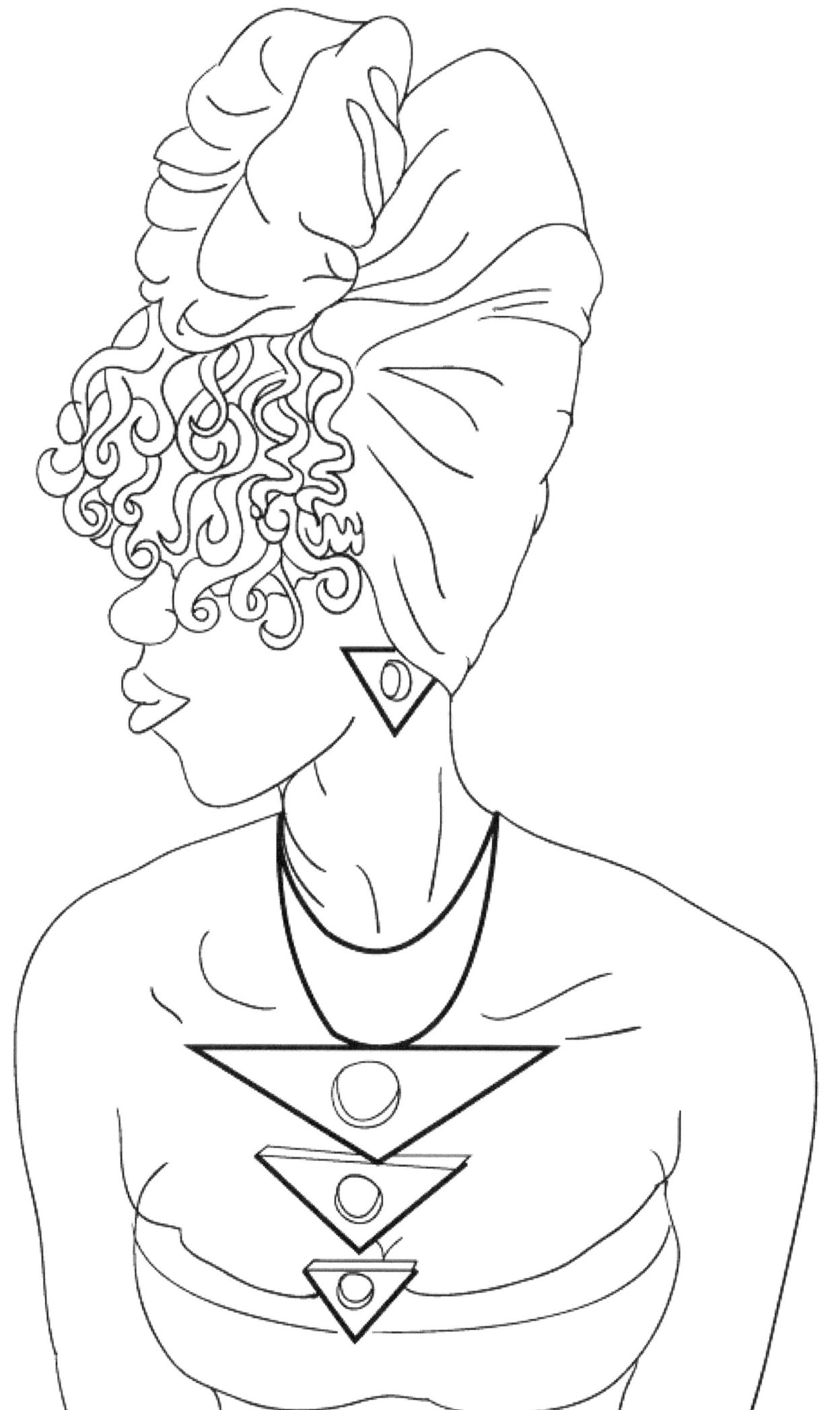

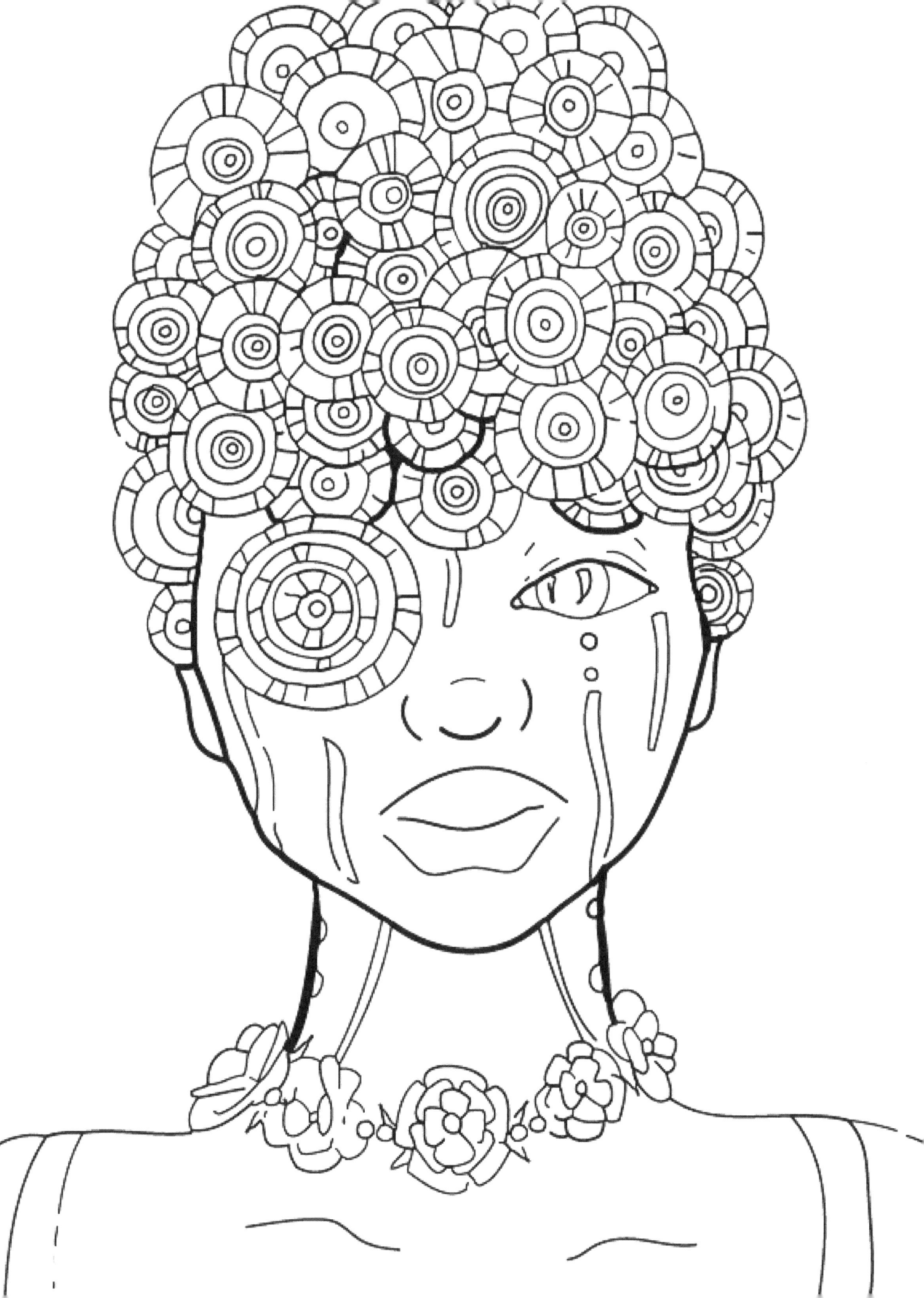

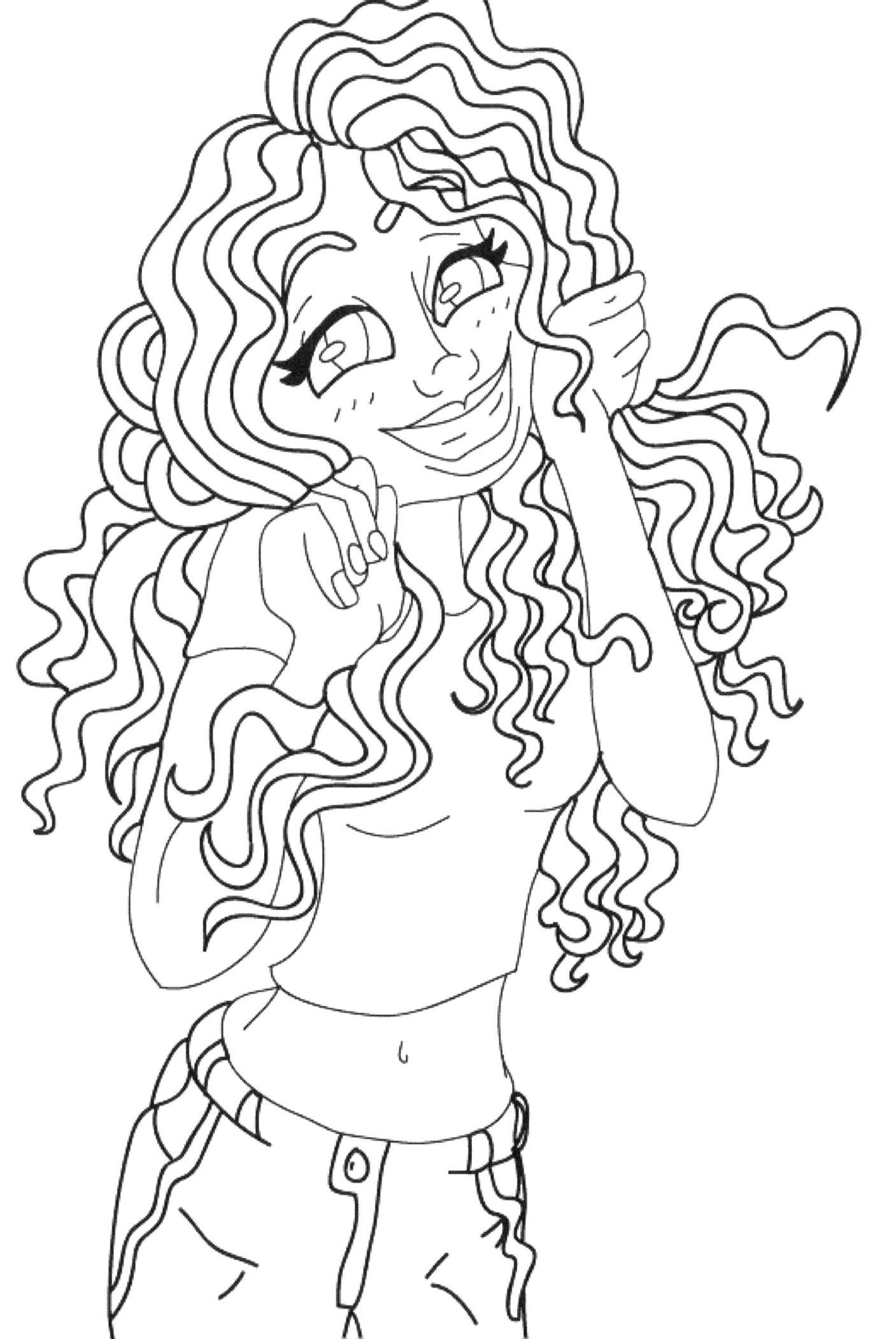

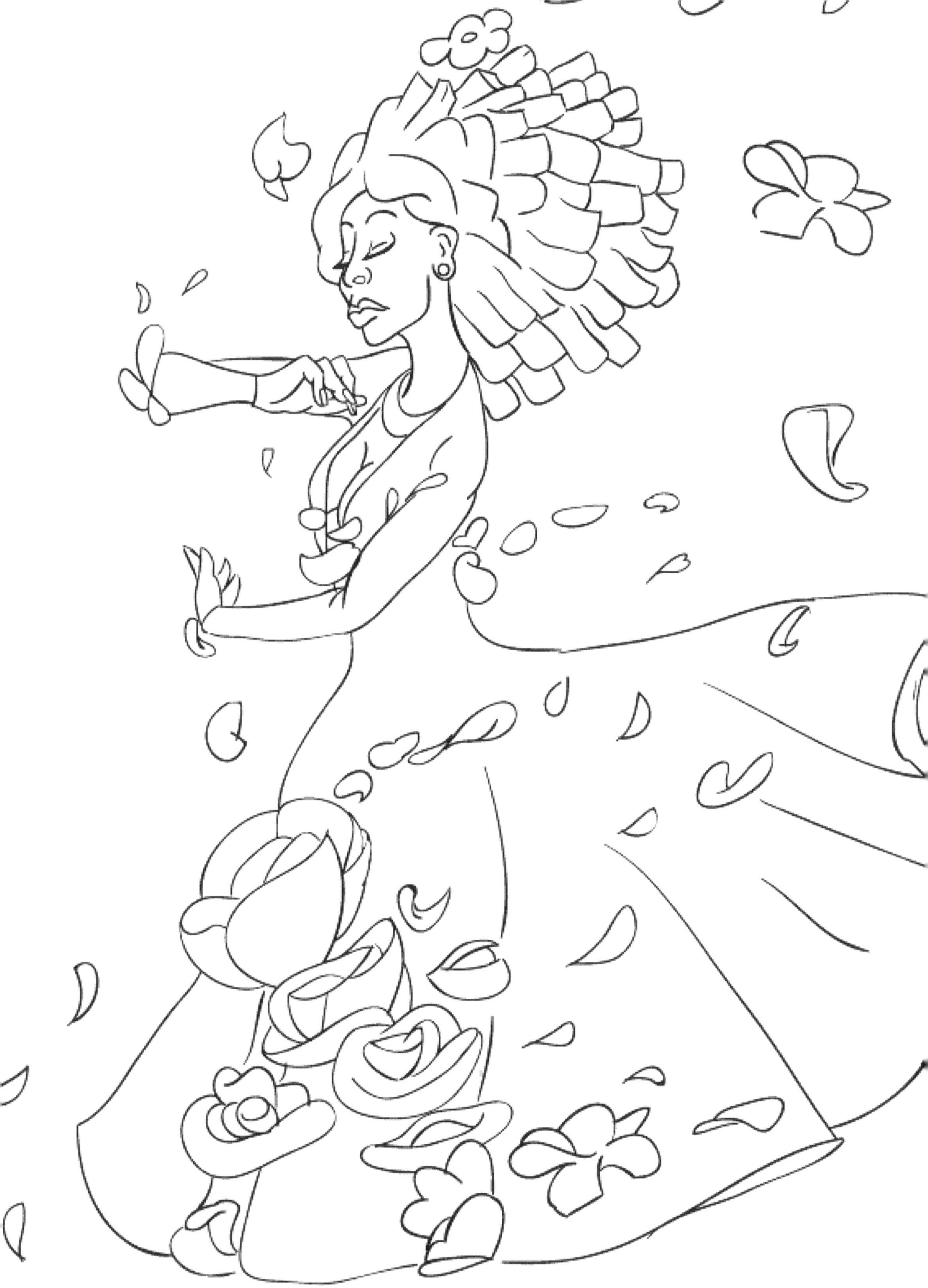

Note from the Artist

Thank you so much! I hope you love coloring these designs as much as I did drawing them.
If you are going to post your finished coloring pages please tag me so I can see them! I just love seeing my designs in color, it just makes my day!

About the Artist

Tyeesha Bradley is a freelance artist from the central Indianapolis area. She has been the feature artist in gallery shows and currently is one of the illustrators for HeartlandNow, an online magazine. While she has done everything from painting murals to designing tattoos, Tyeesha's real love is character design. She is an unrepentant BLERD or black nerd and will talk your ear off about manga, anime, fantasy books, and board games. And yes, she will be at EVERY premiere of super hero films, no matter how bad they are.
You can connect with Tyeesha on Facebook at facebook.com/tyeeshabradleystudio,
Etsy.com/shop/tyeeshabradleystudio, or Instagram @tyeeshabradley.
Go ahead and follow while you're at it!